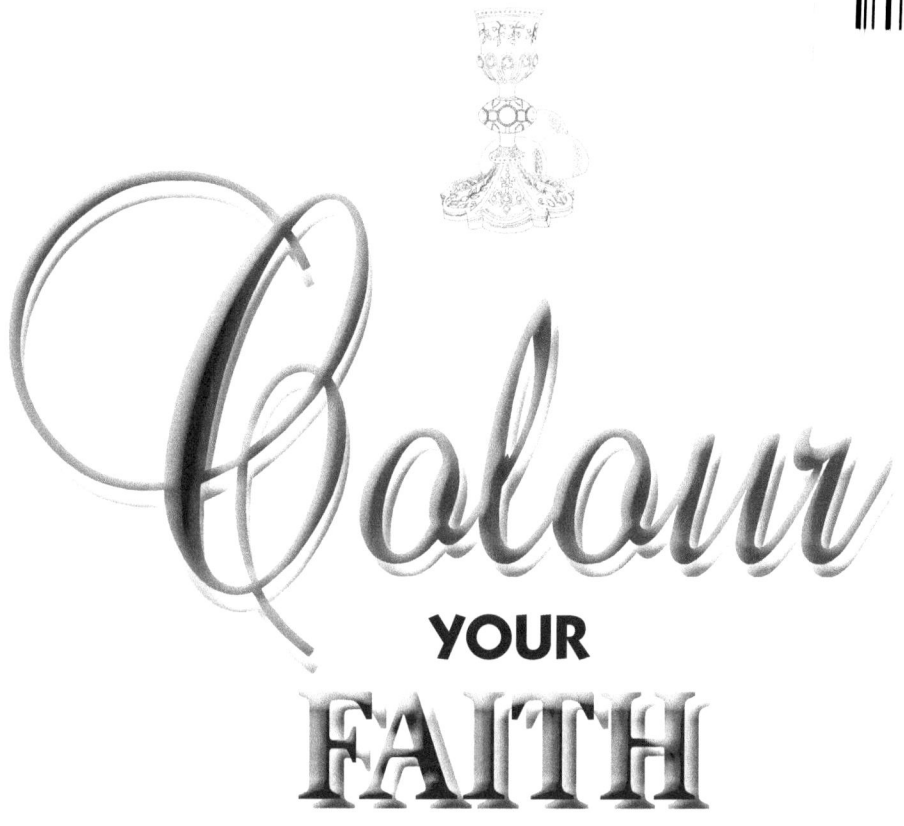

Colour
YOUR
FAITH

DRAWINGS

BY

KAY MARIE ENNS

An inspiring adult colouring experience
of 76 original drawings of traditional
and modern symbols of Christian belief.

Published by:

Normetha Publications
Winnipeg, Manitoba, Canada

ISBN-10: 1523715774
ISBN-13: 9781523715770

All drawings and cover paintings: Kay Marie Enns
Text pages and cover design: George Wolfe Friesen

Published by:

Normetha Publications
Winnipeg, Manitoba, Canada

To Begin With

Colour Your Faith is a book featuring remarkable drawings of the signatures and signs of the Christian faith. We have taken some of the cherished symbols and monograms and refashioned them, giving them a bit of hutzpah and setting them into fresh frameworks and new poses— poses that still serve to make the ancient hooks upon which we hang our faith relevant and compelling.

We present this unique collection to you as a garden of delight, a feast of hope and the substance of faith.

• Enter your faith by bringing each of the images here into the richness of dazzling colour.

• Colour while you contemplate the awesome richness of the church's treasury of belief.

• Celebrate this unrestrained jamboree of the symbols that form the "house language" of the church.

• Follow your creative instincts; relax and de-stress your mind and body.

• Reward yourself with a finished portfolio of beautiful artwork.

• Soothe your soul; be playful as you put earthly matters to rest.

All in all, let this book of drawings refresh and bring your faith deeper into the realm of experience.

Go for it, and have fun.

— KME

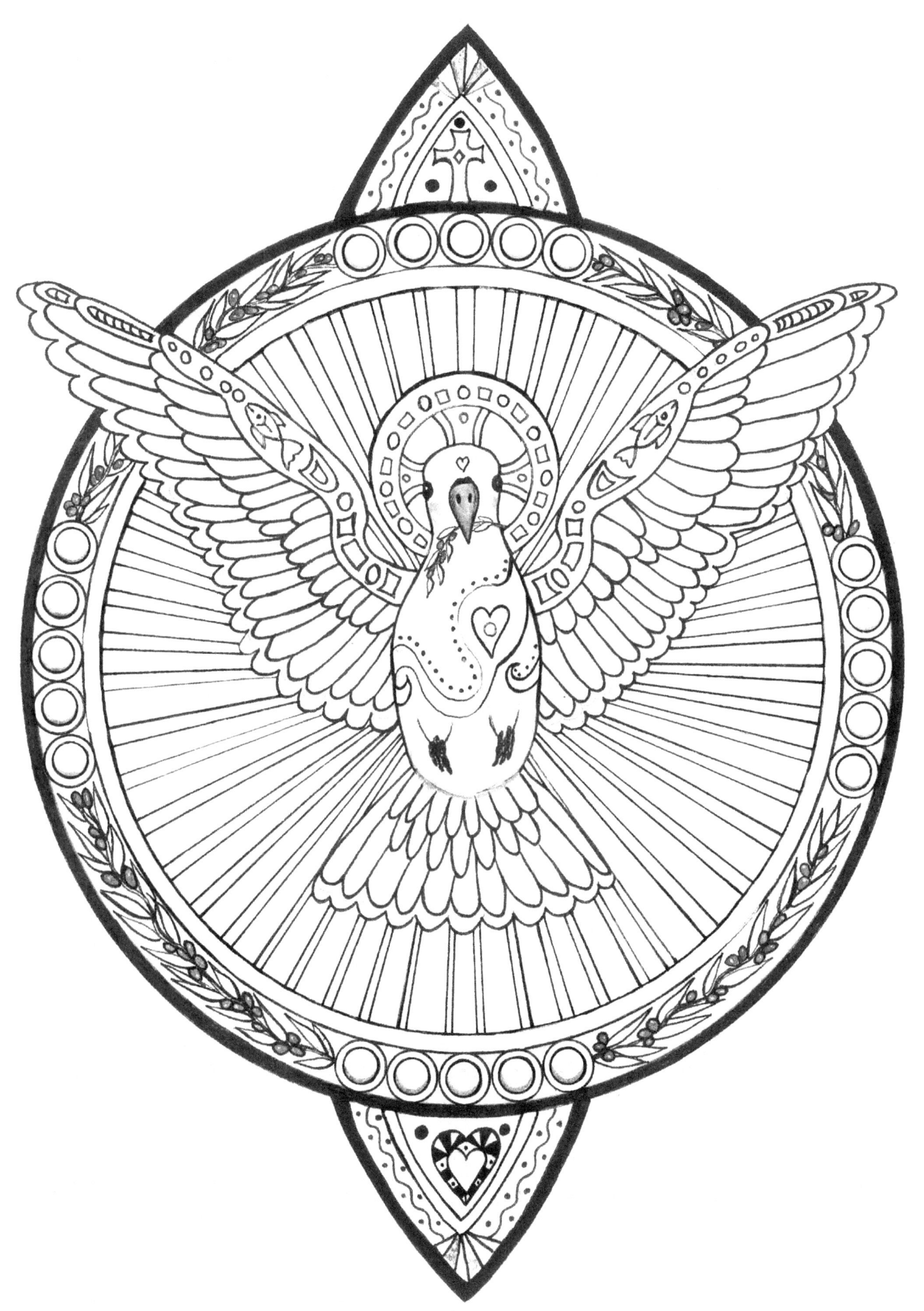

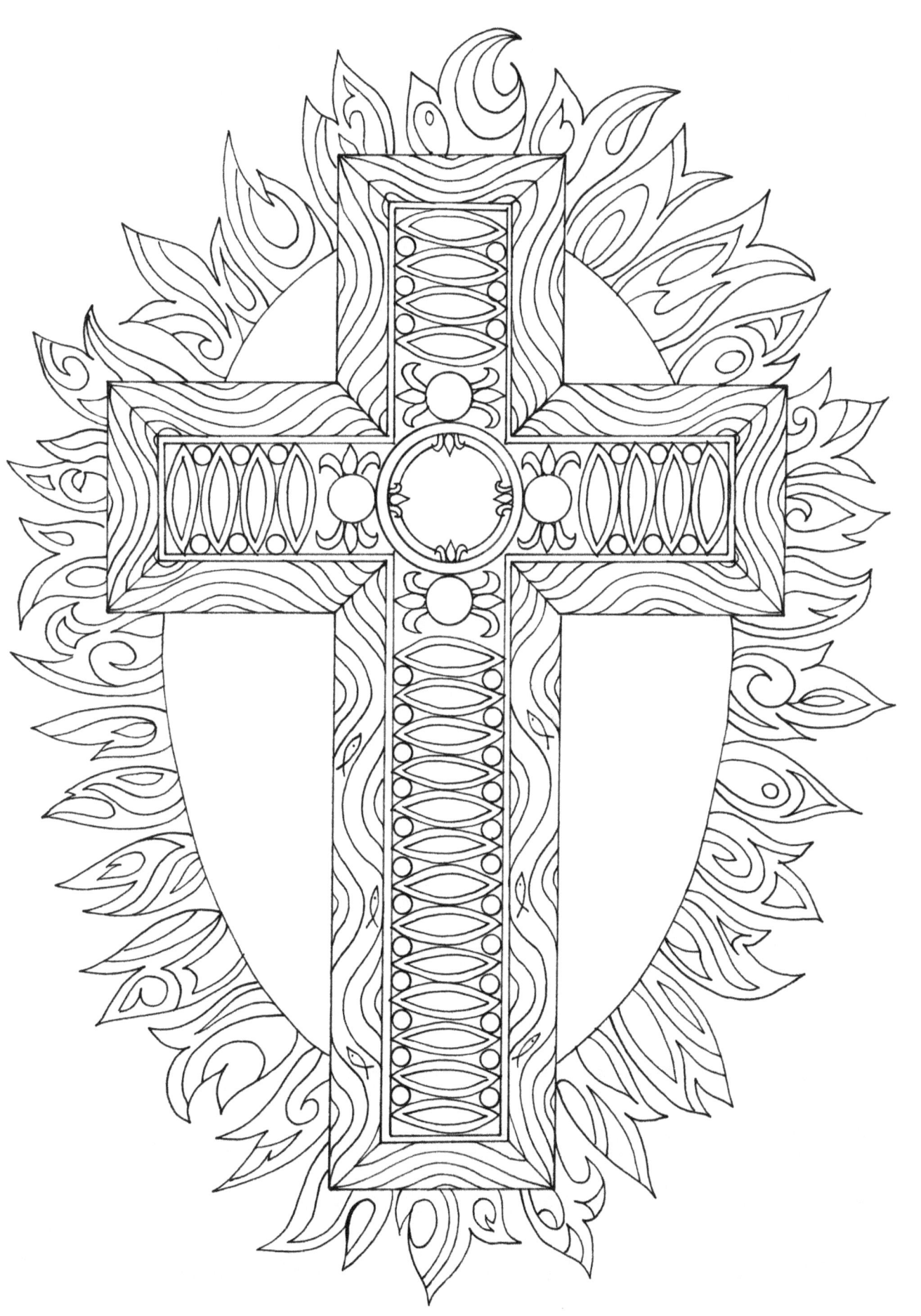

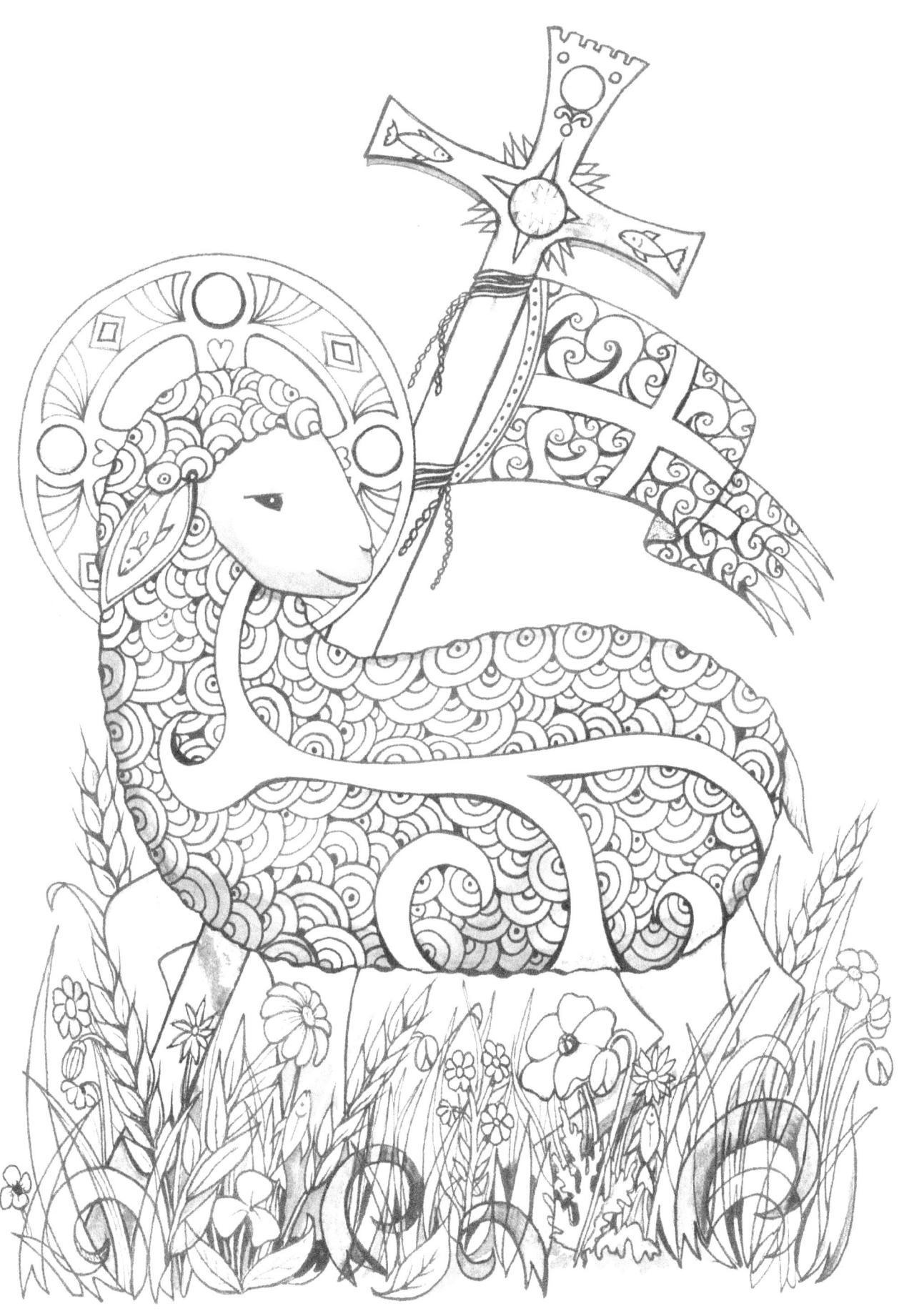

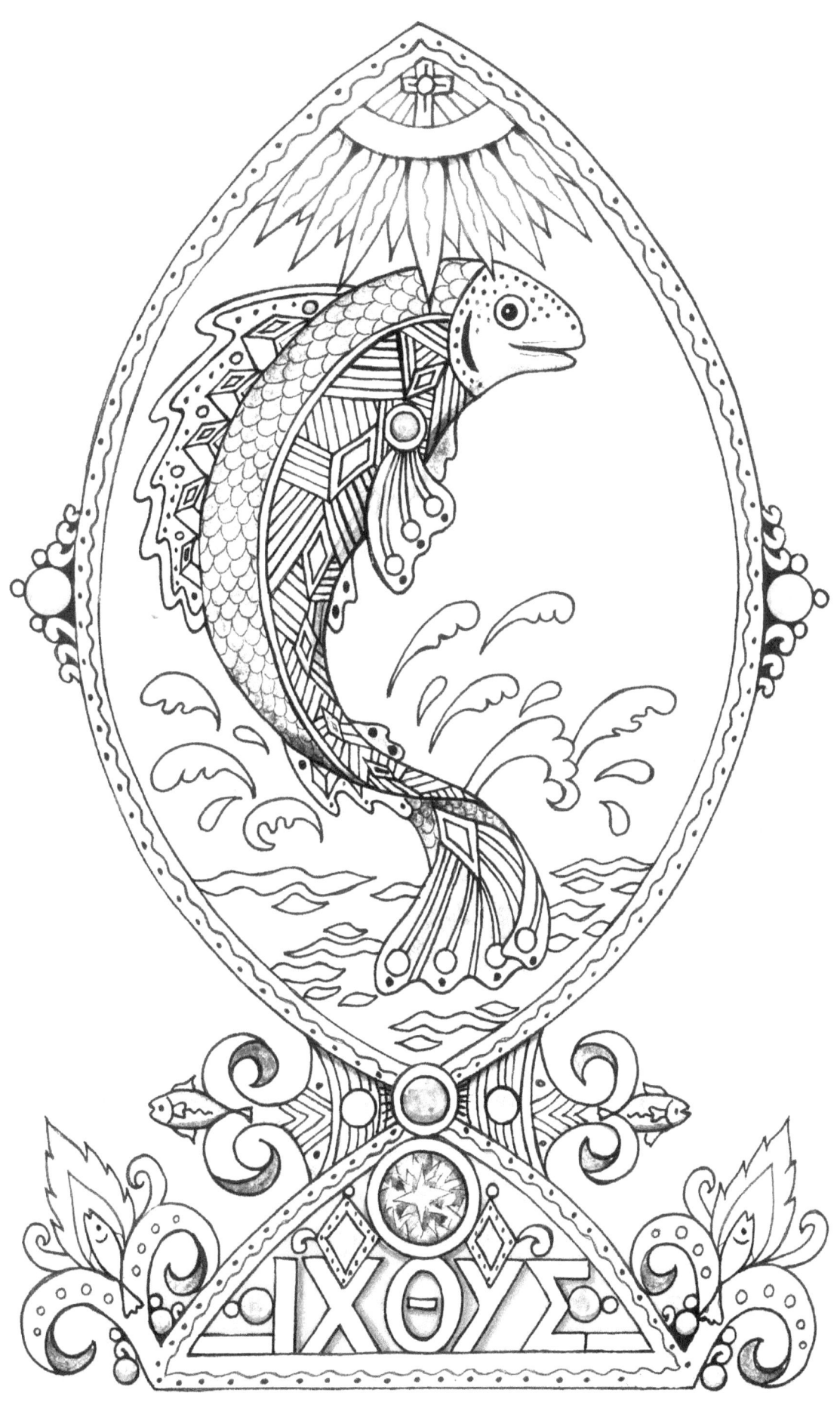

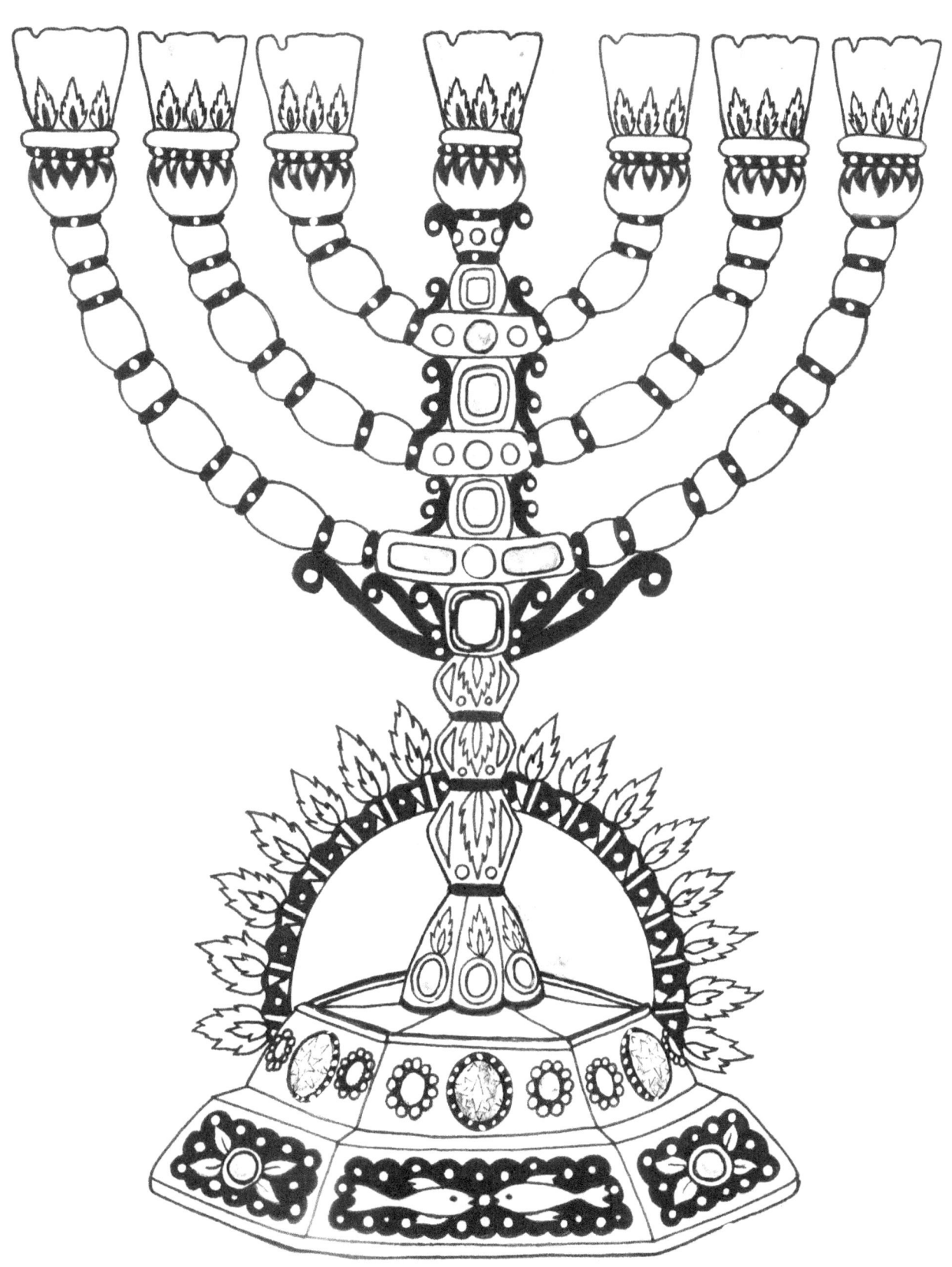

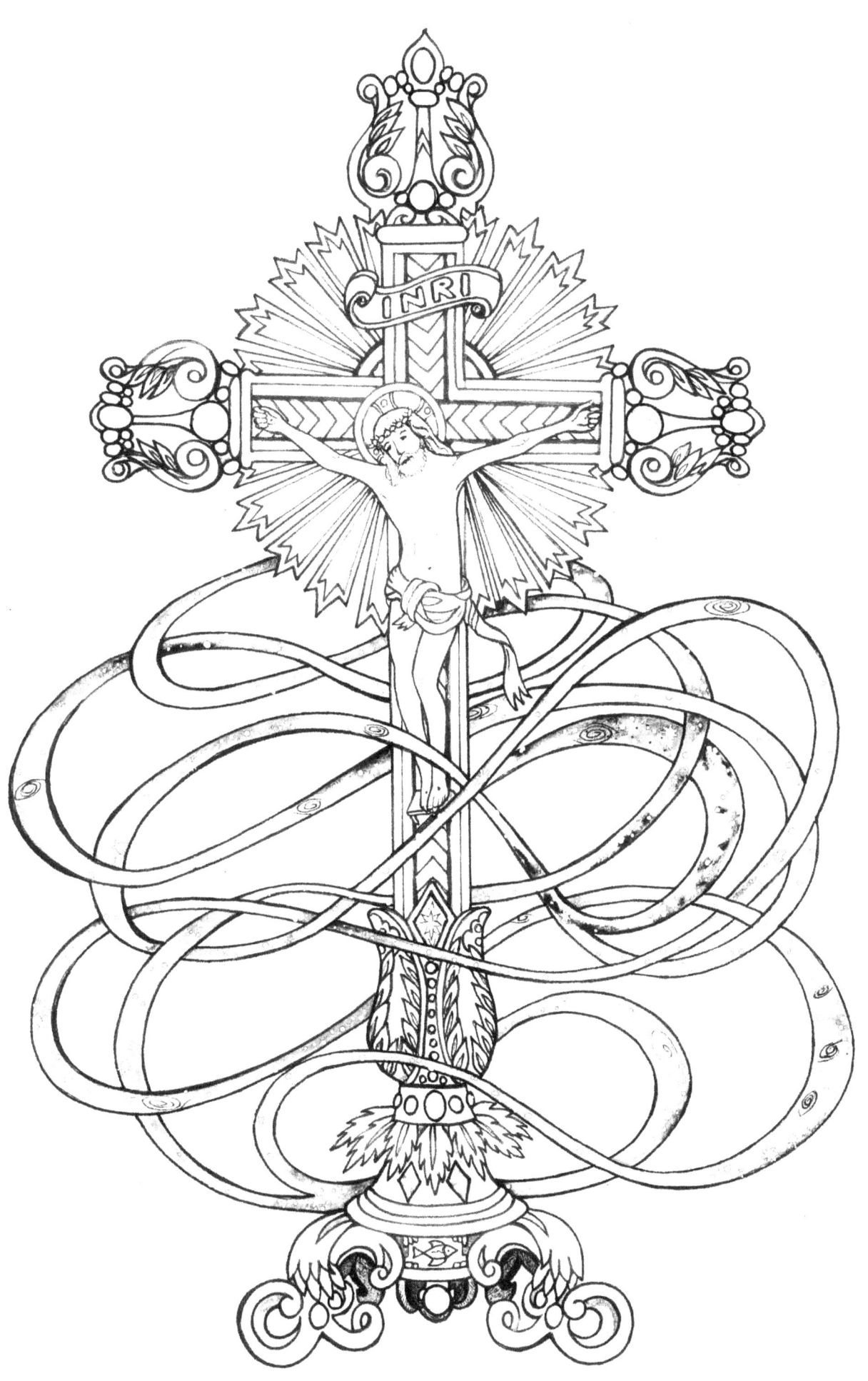

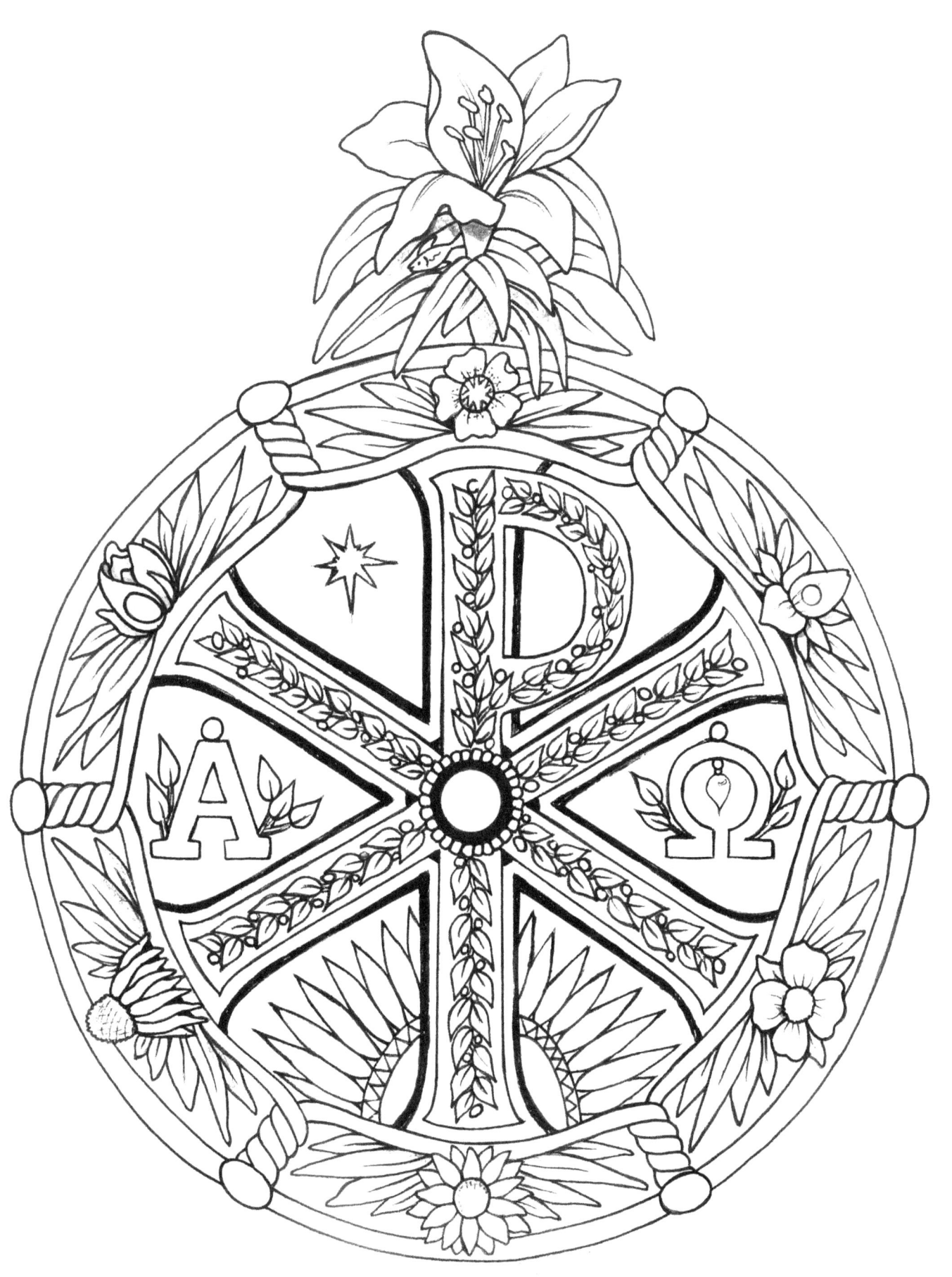

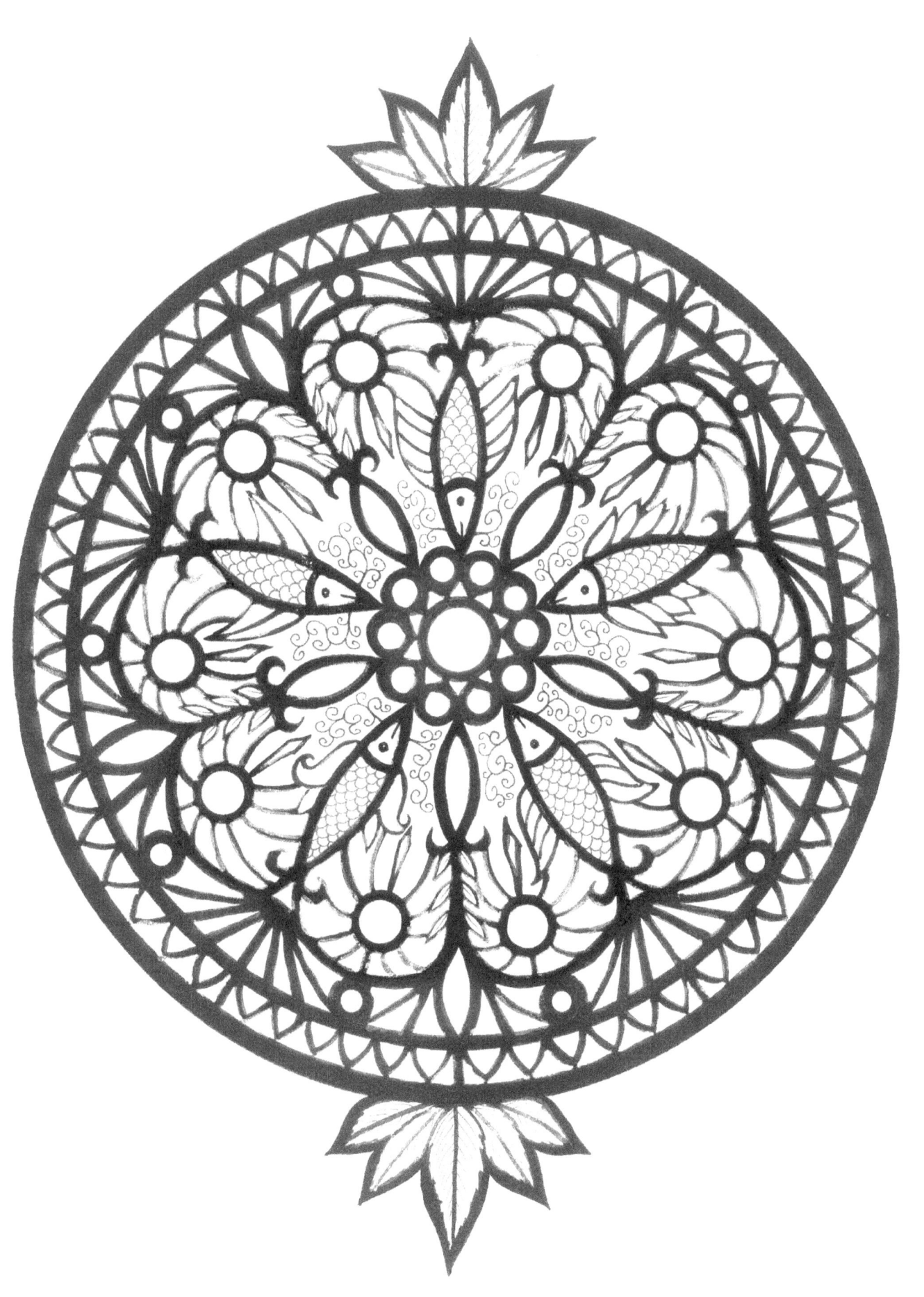

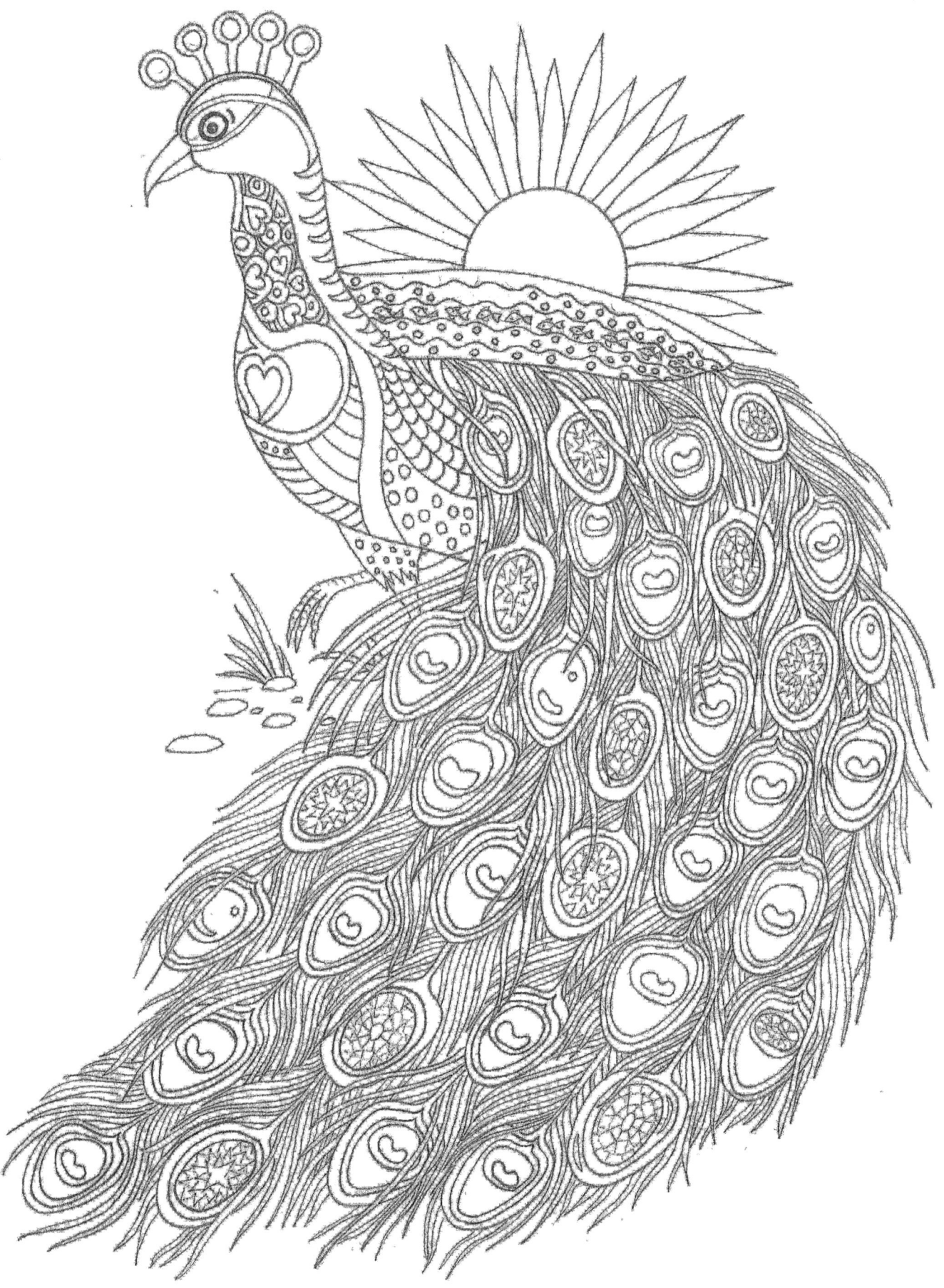

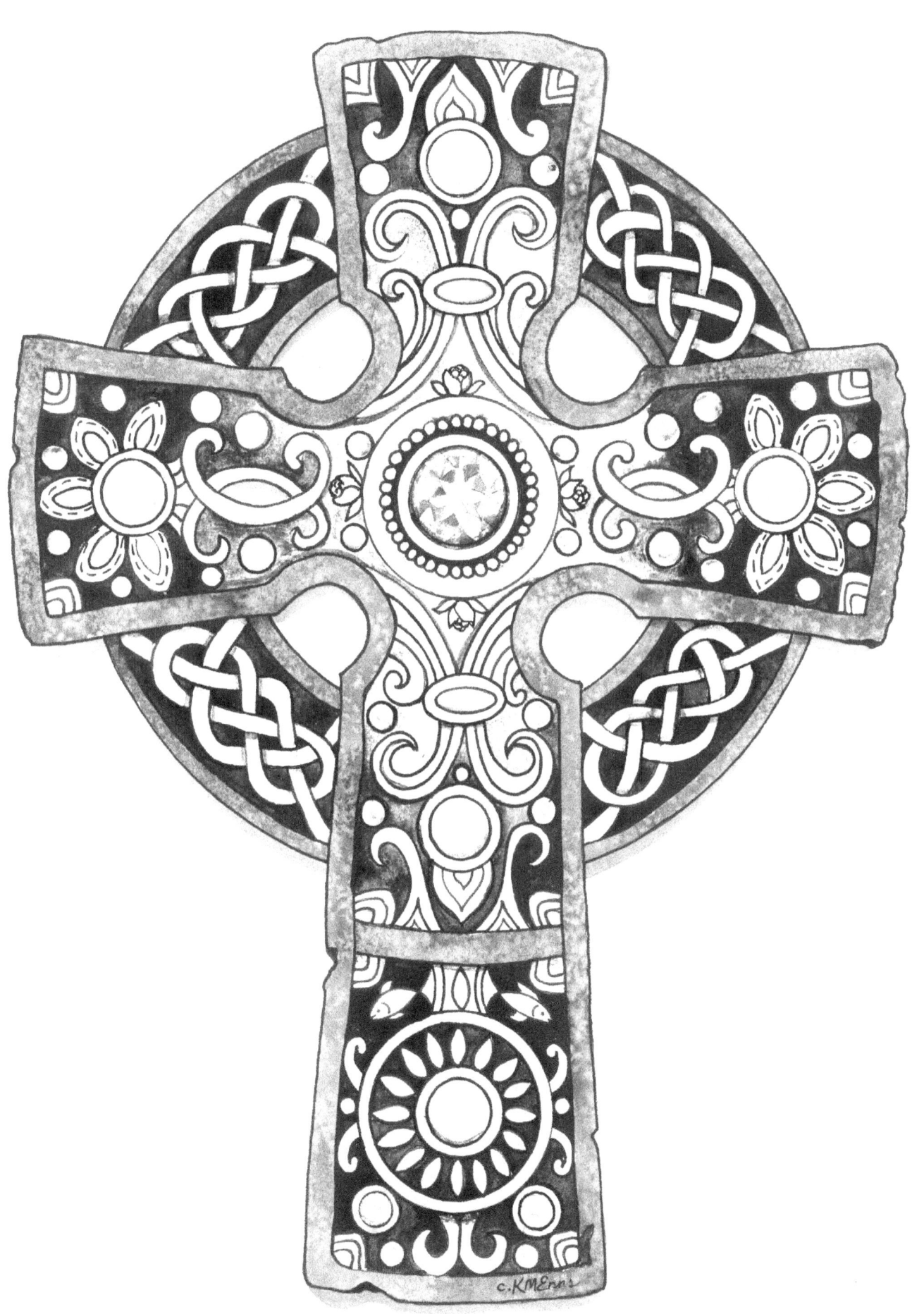

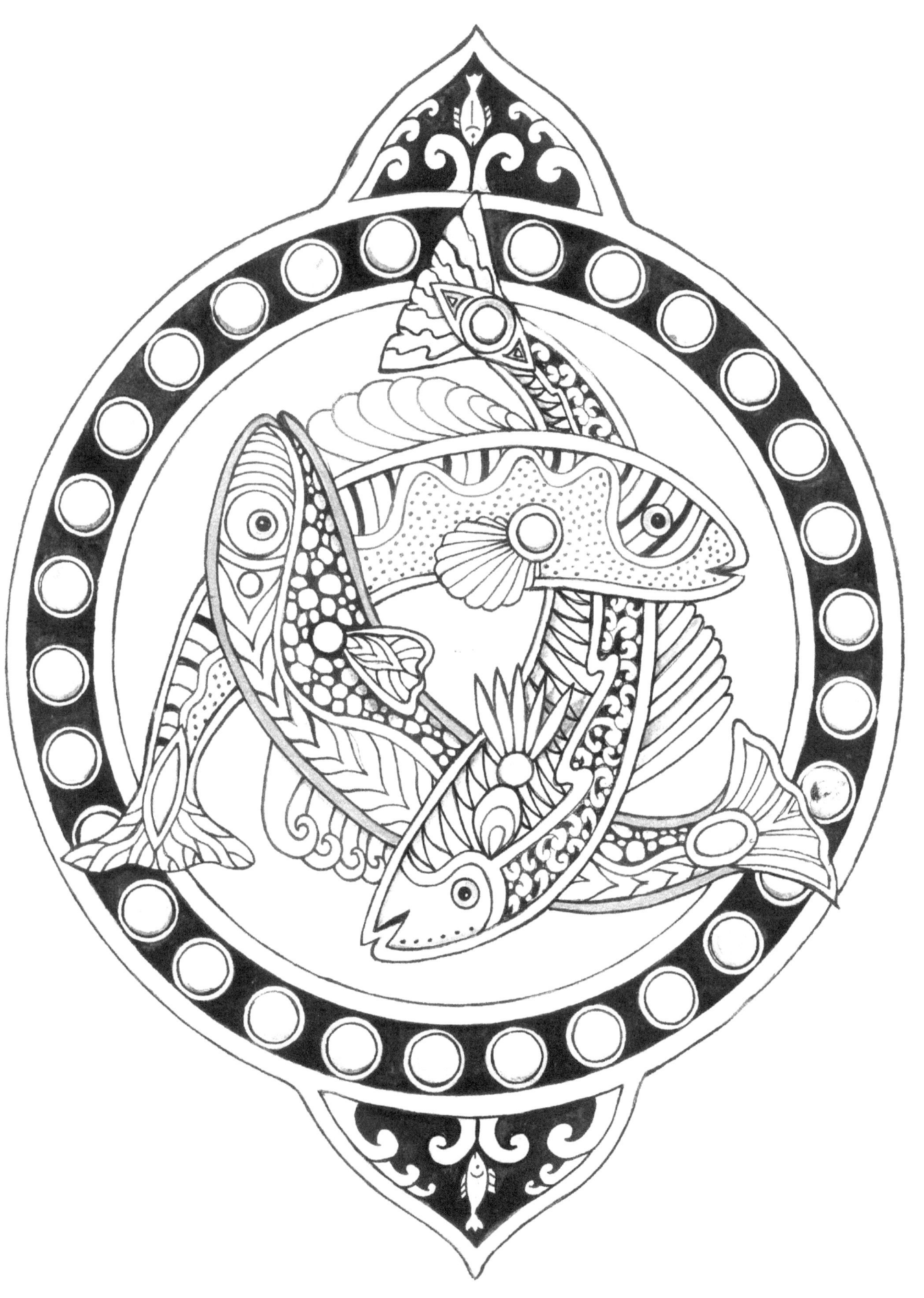

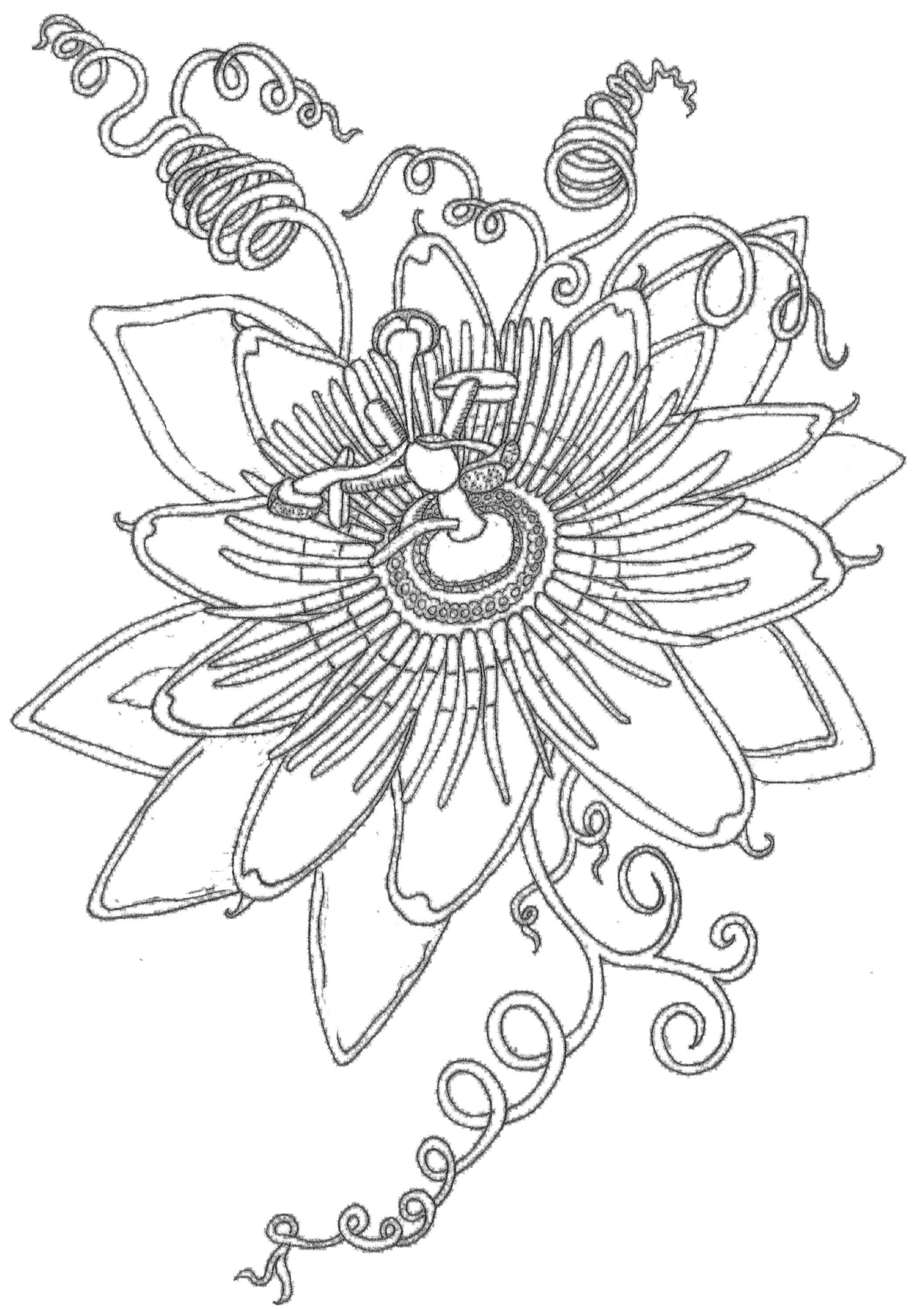

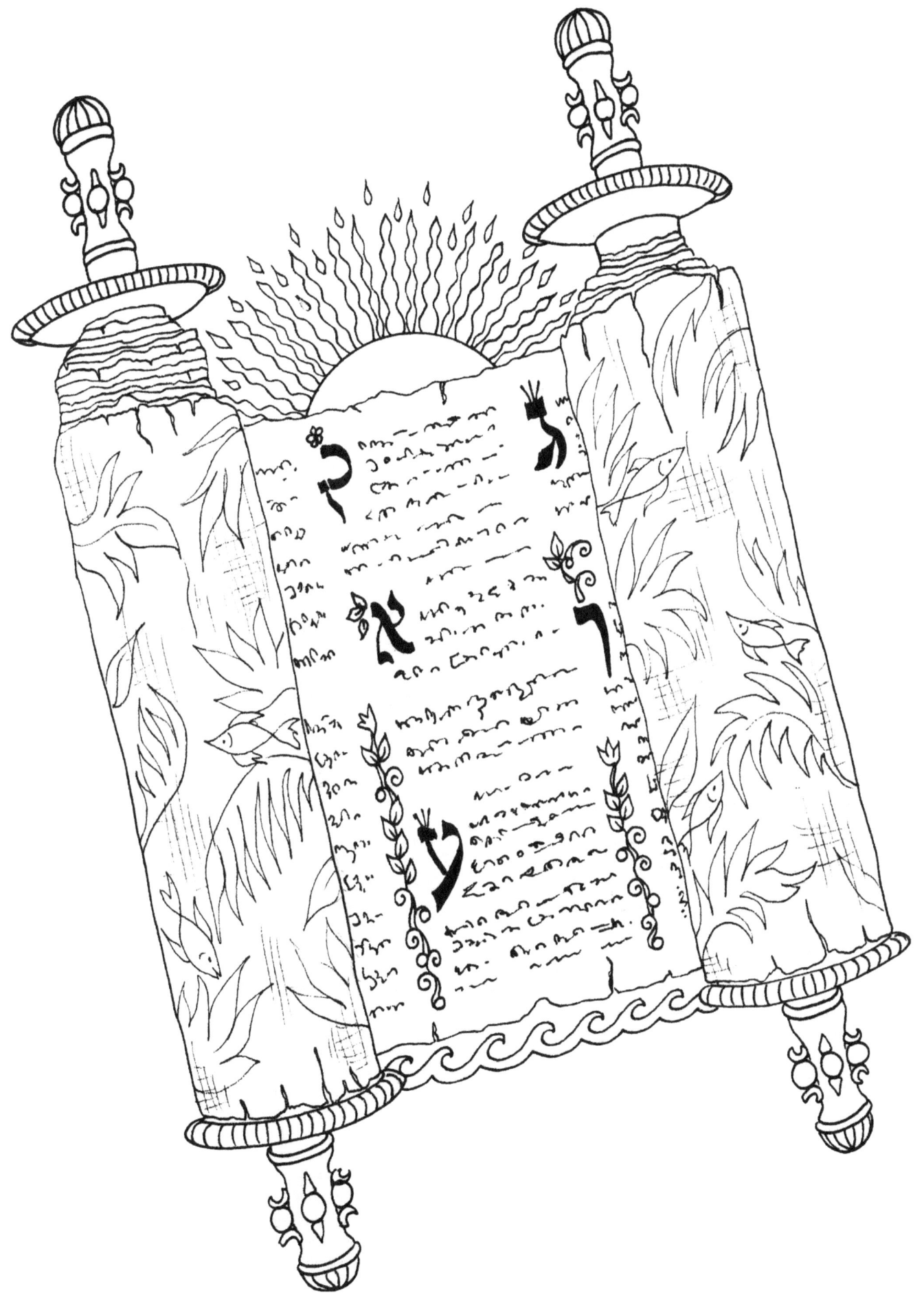

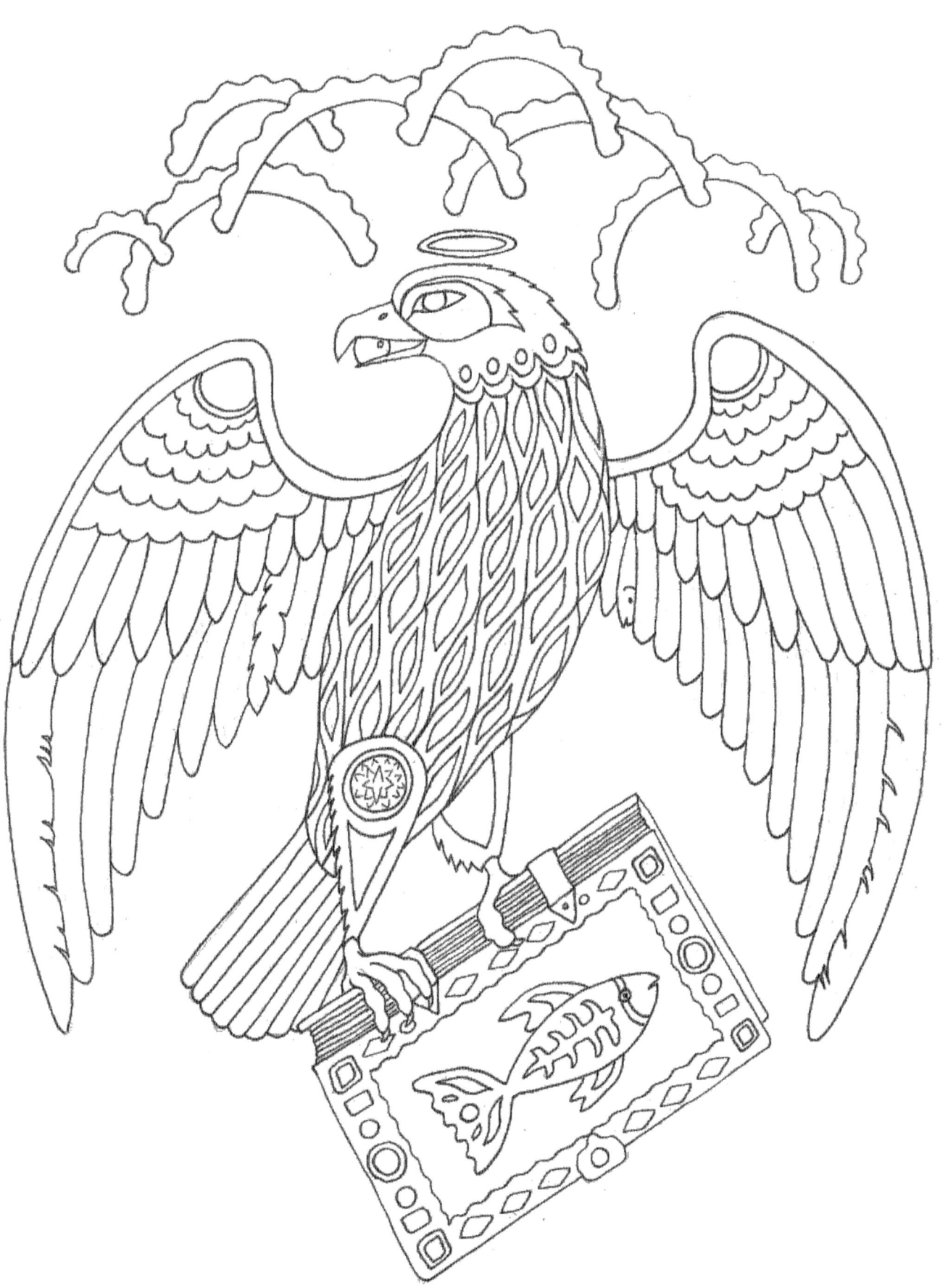

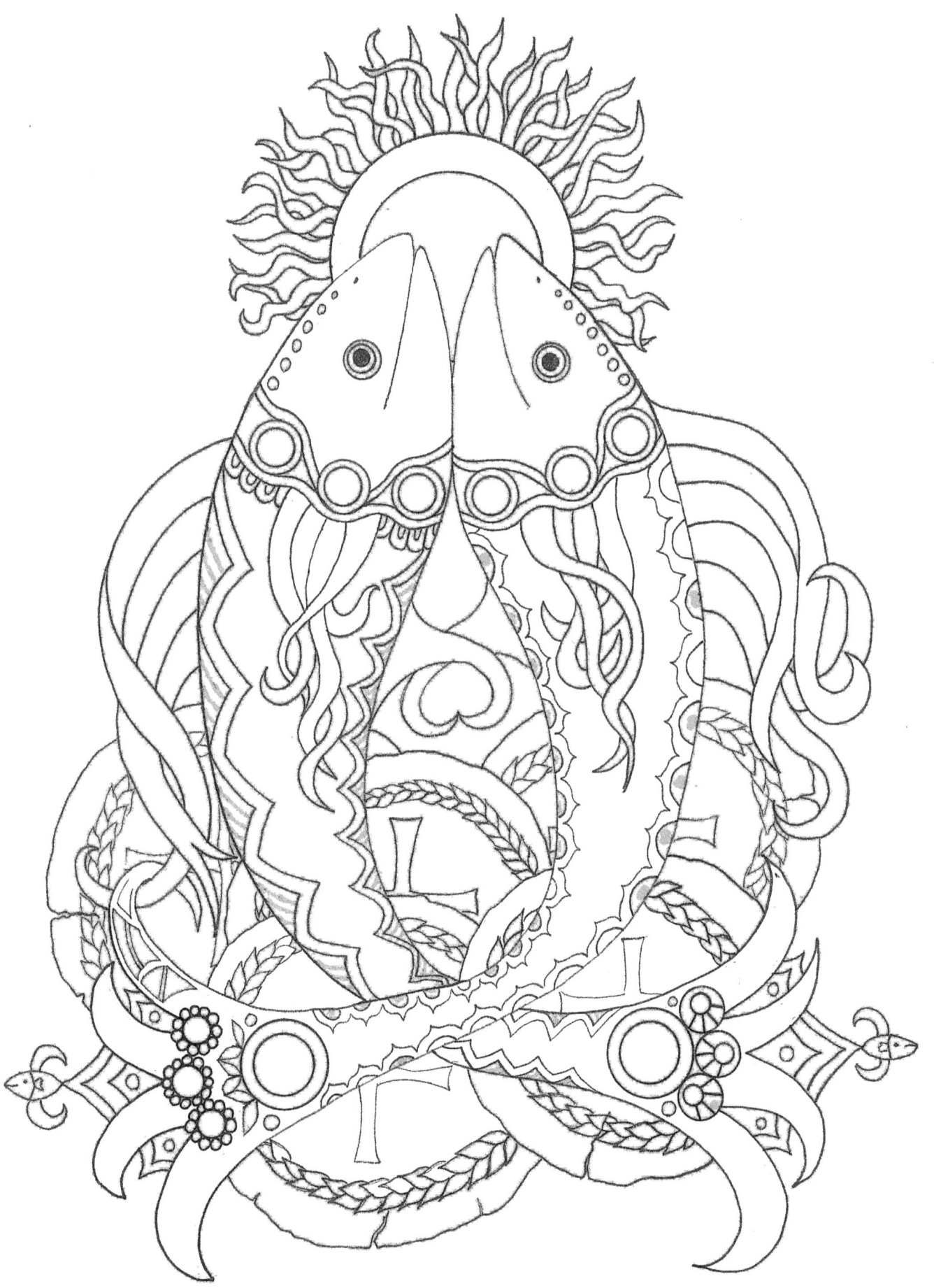

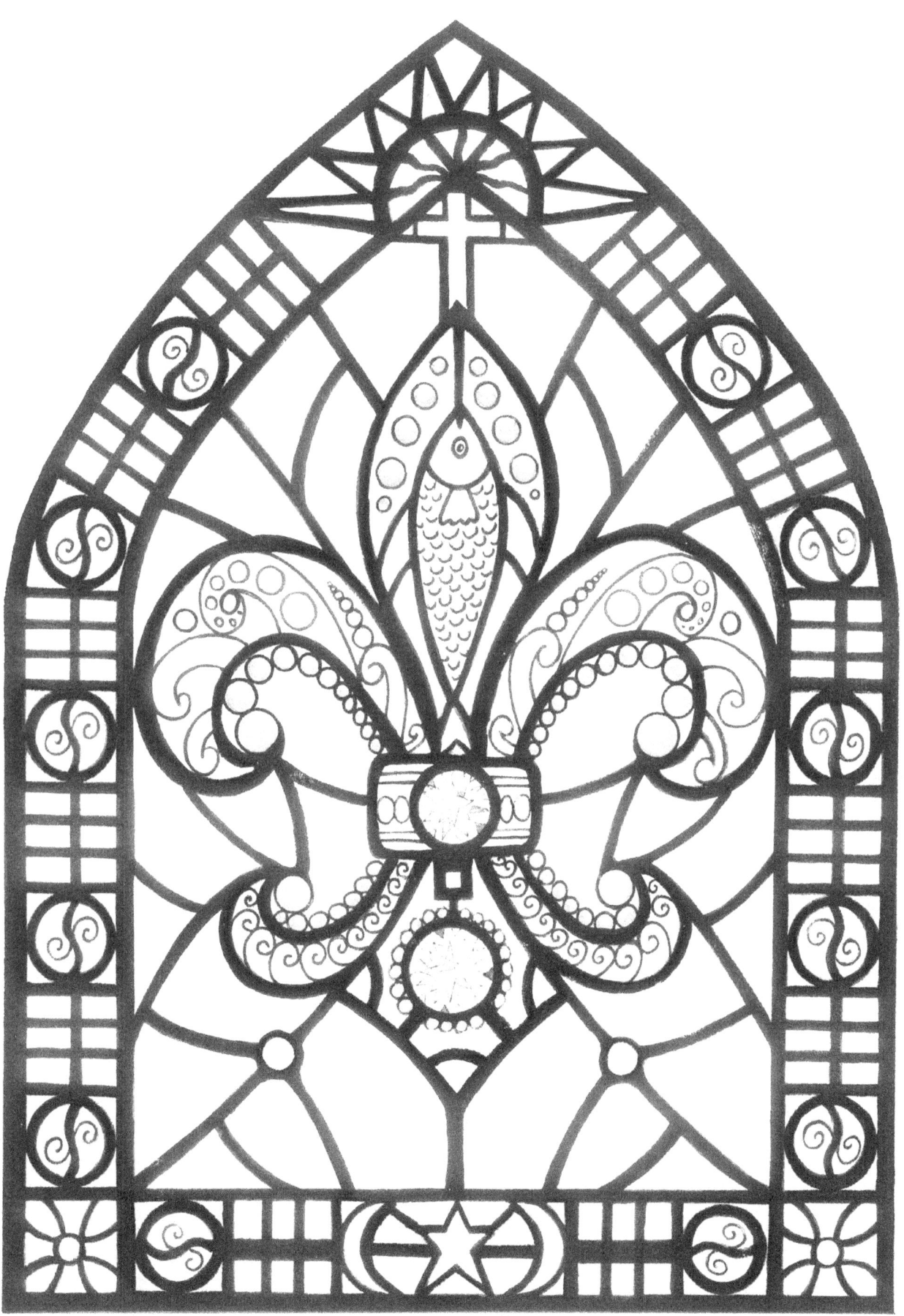

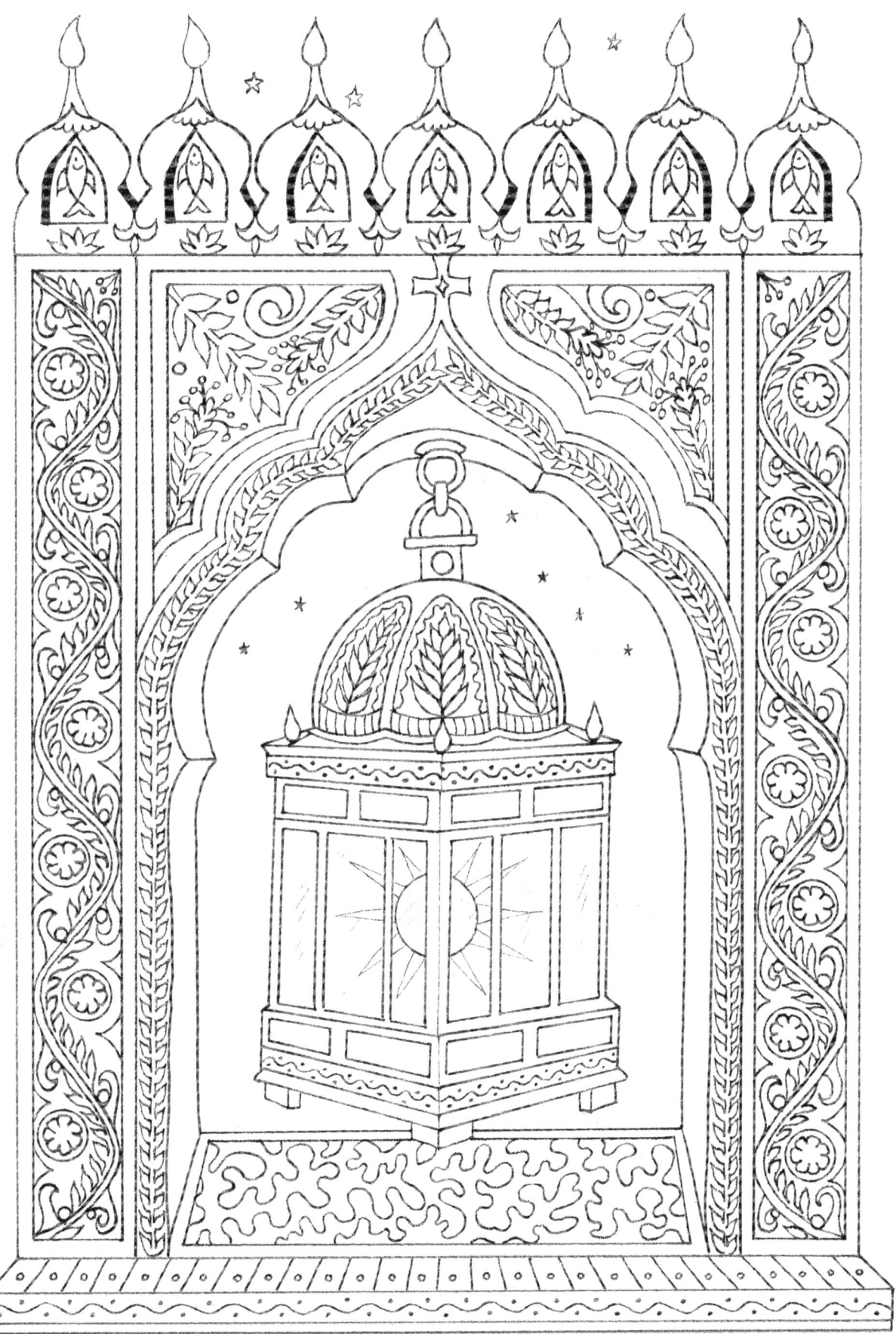

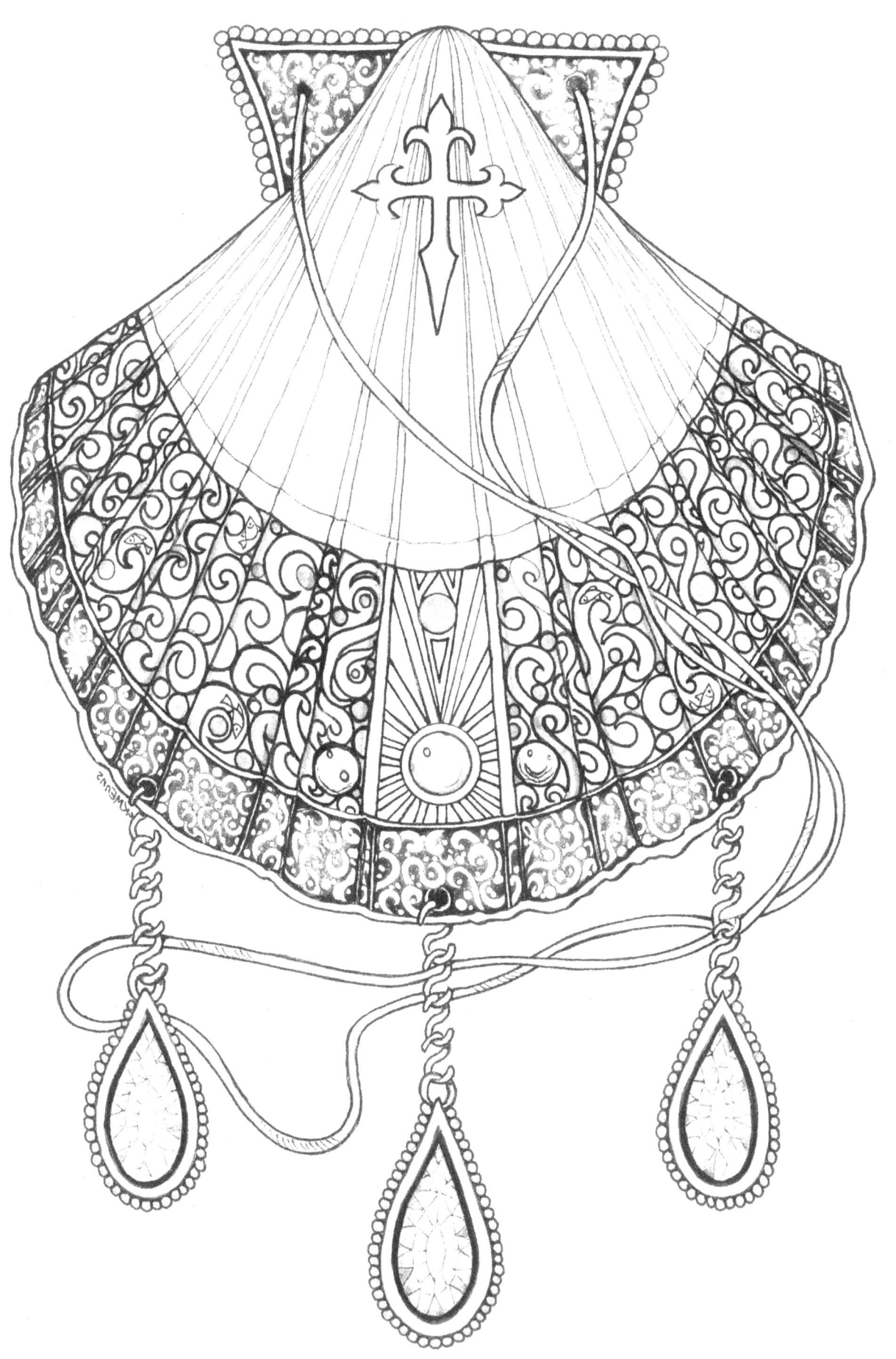

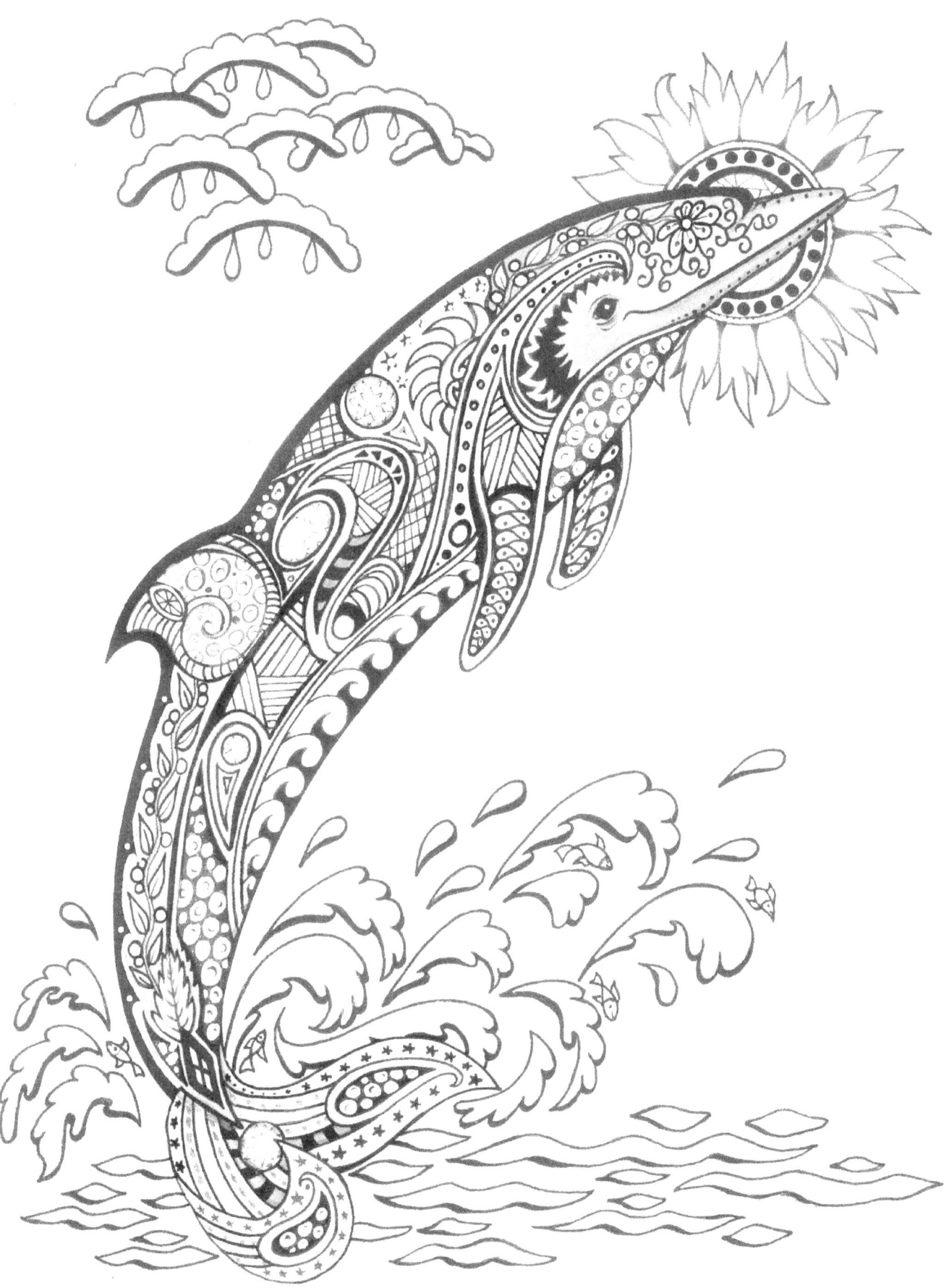

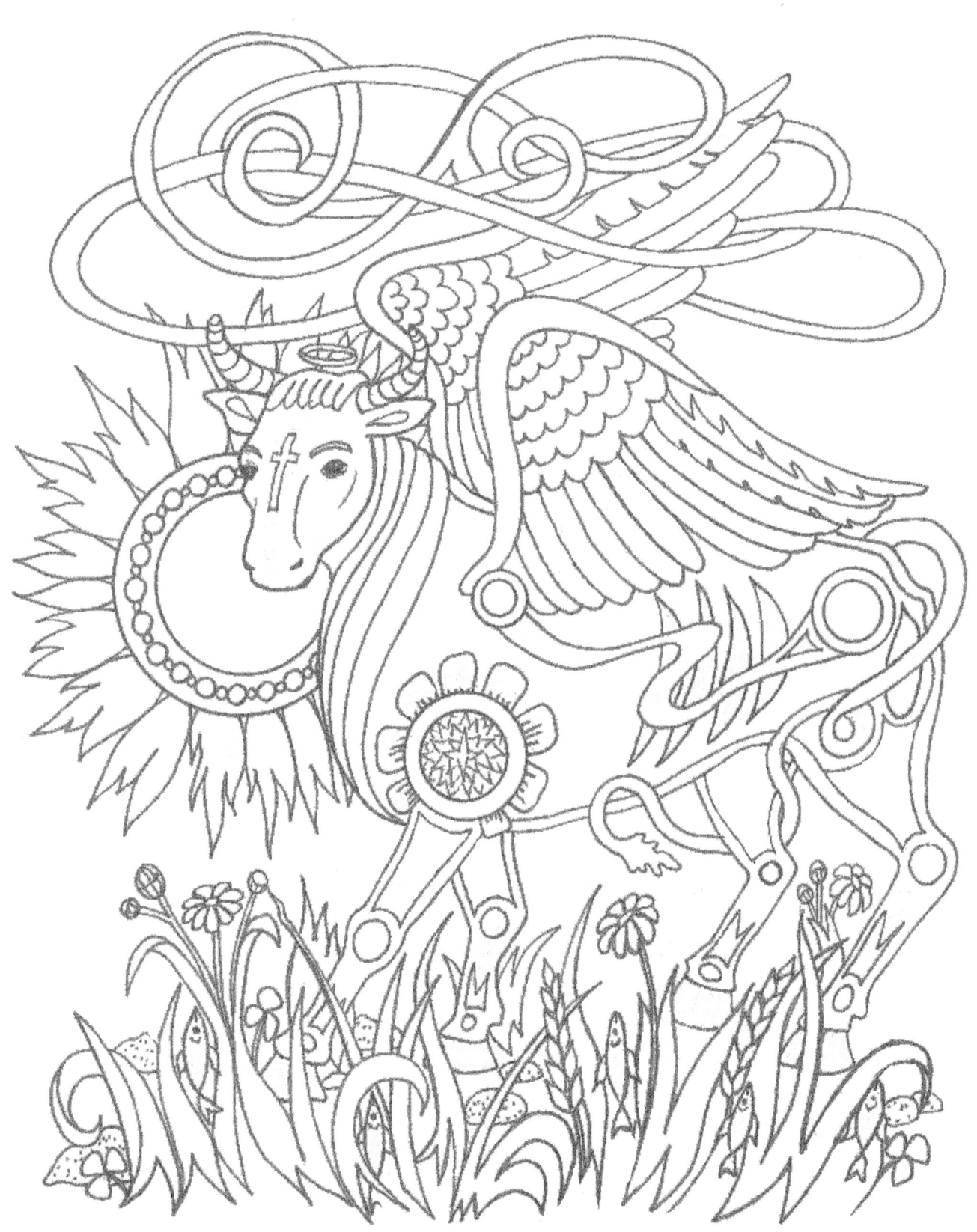

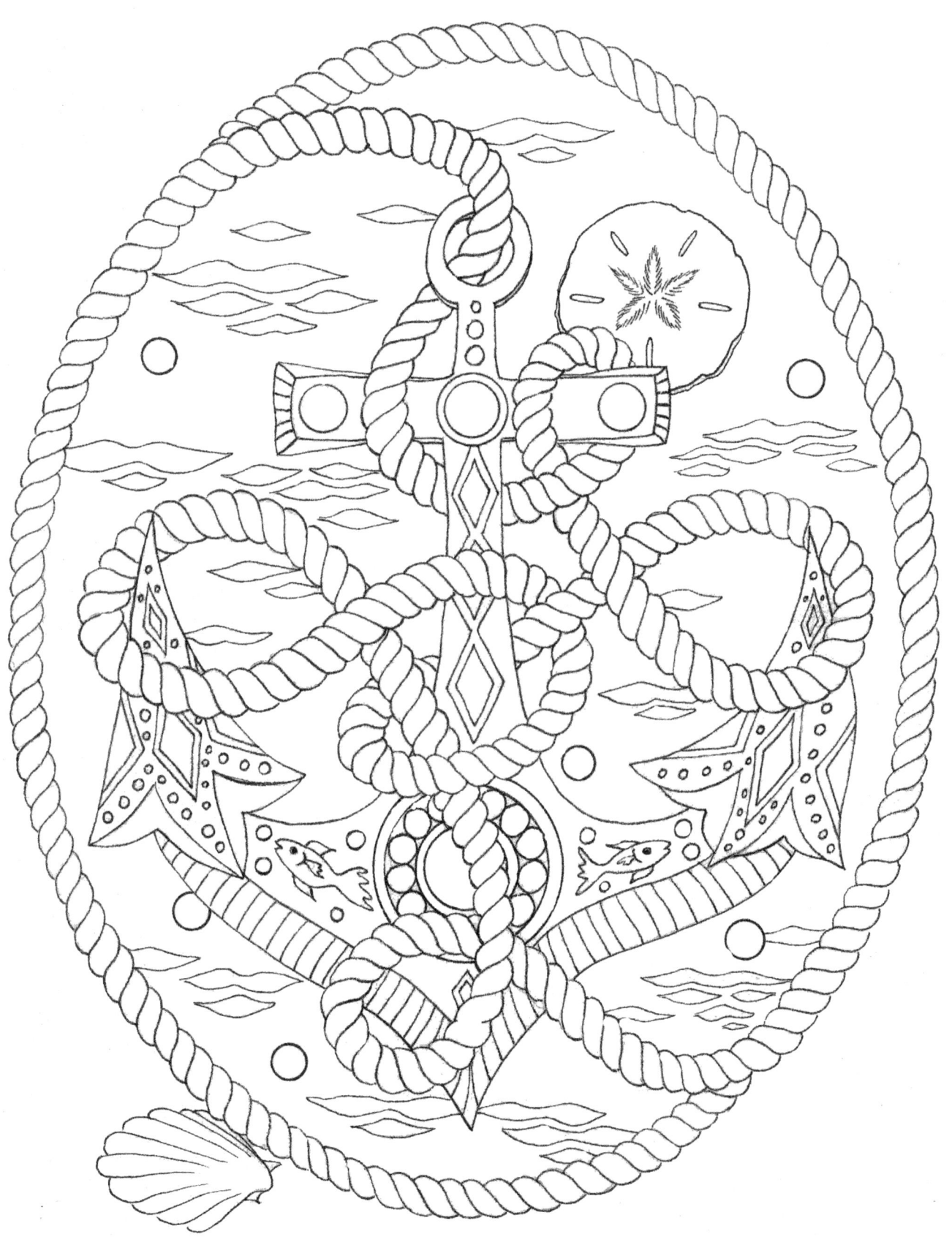

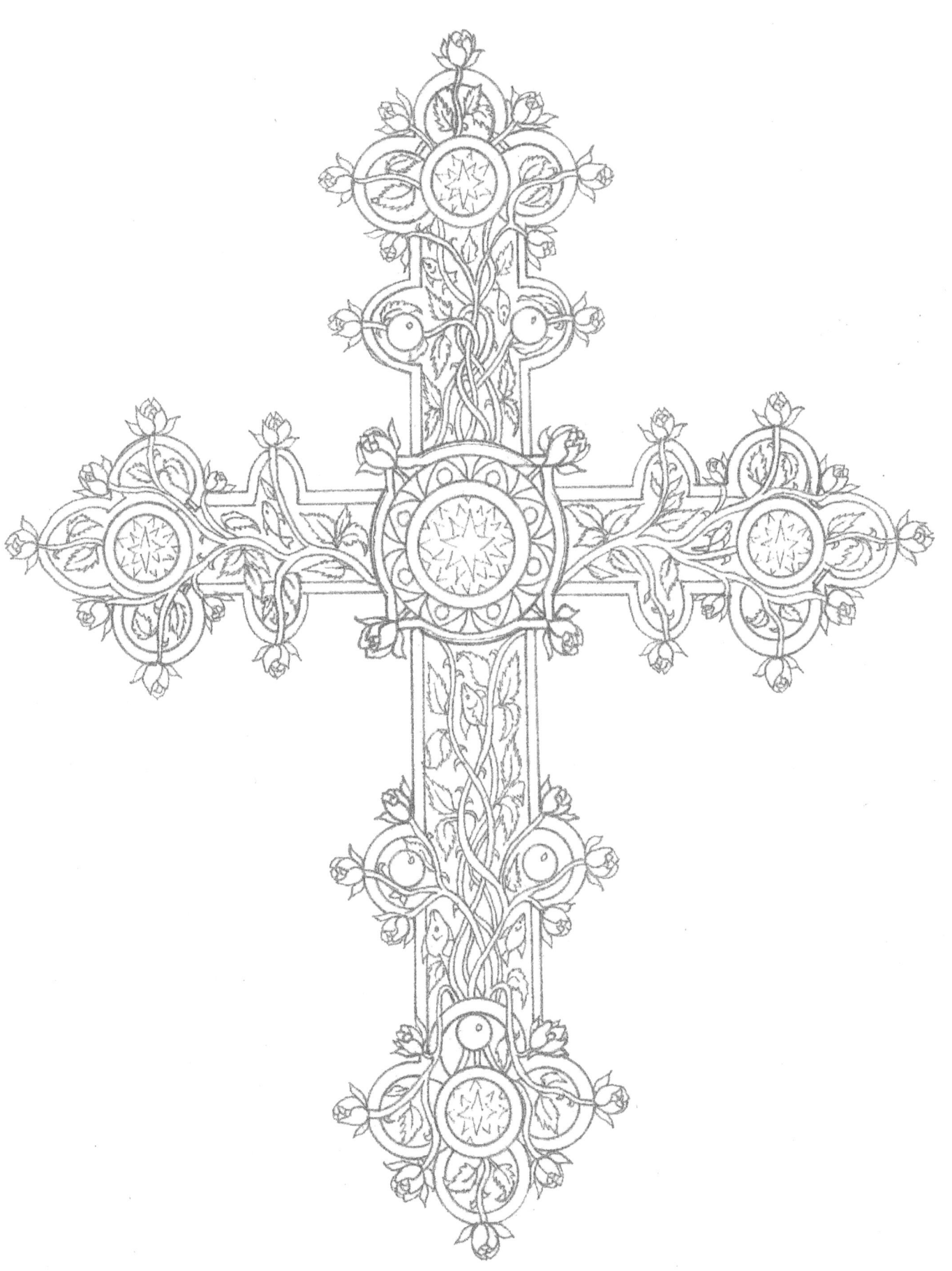

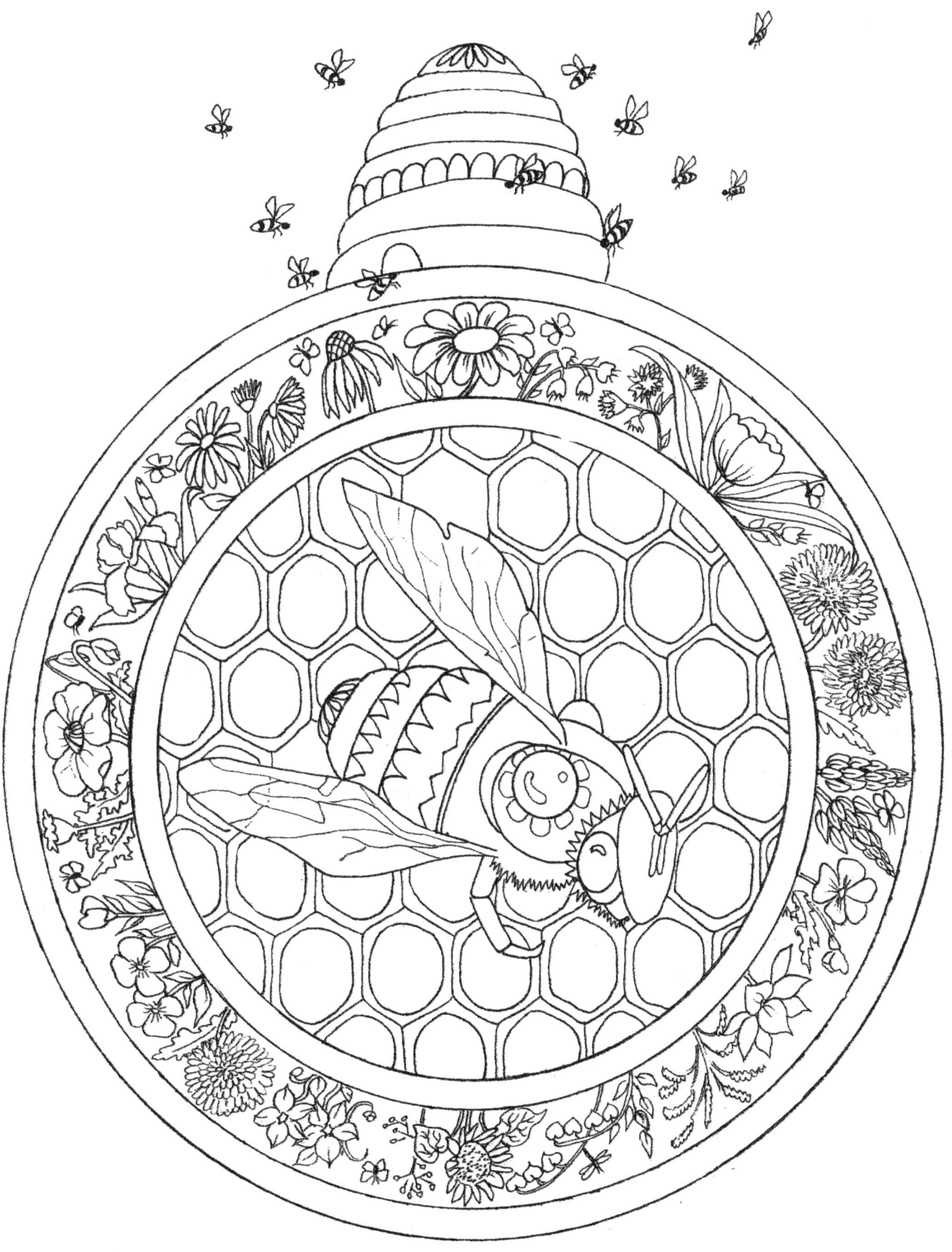

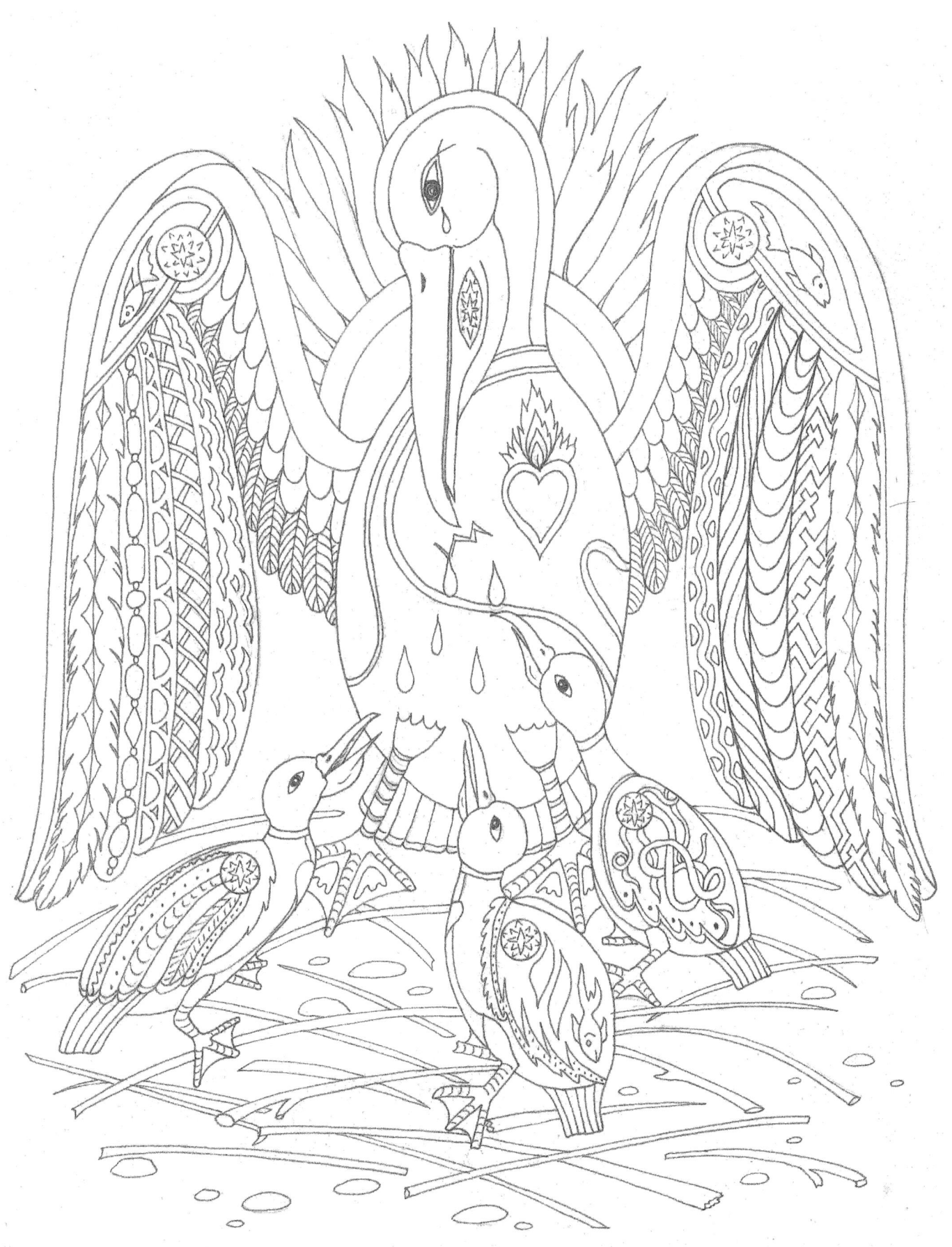

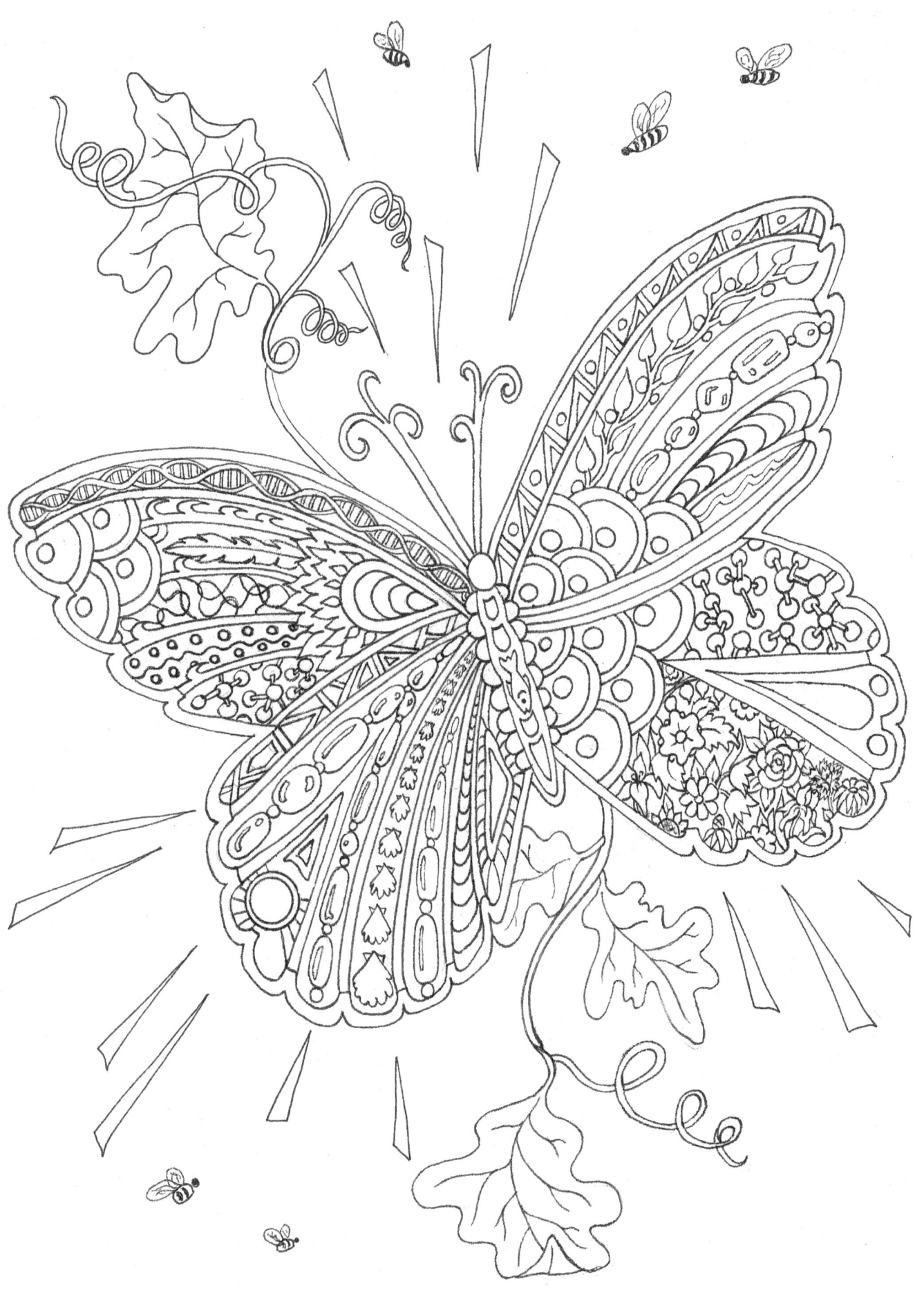

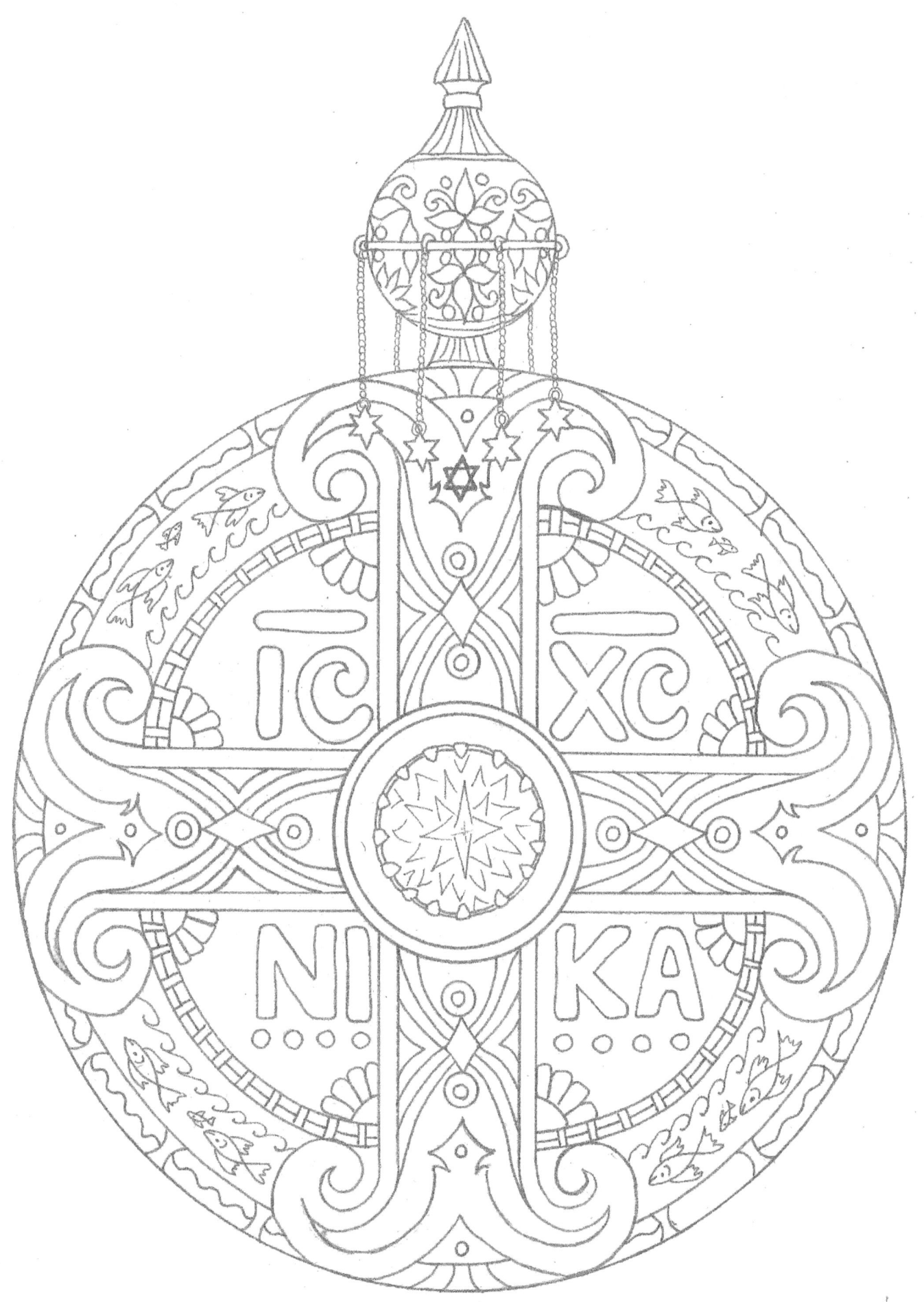

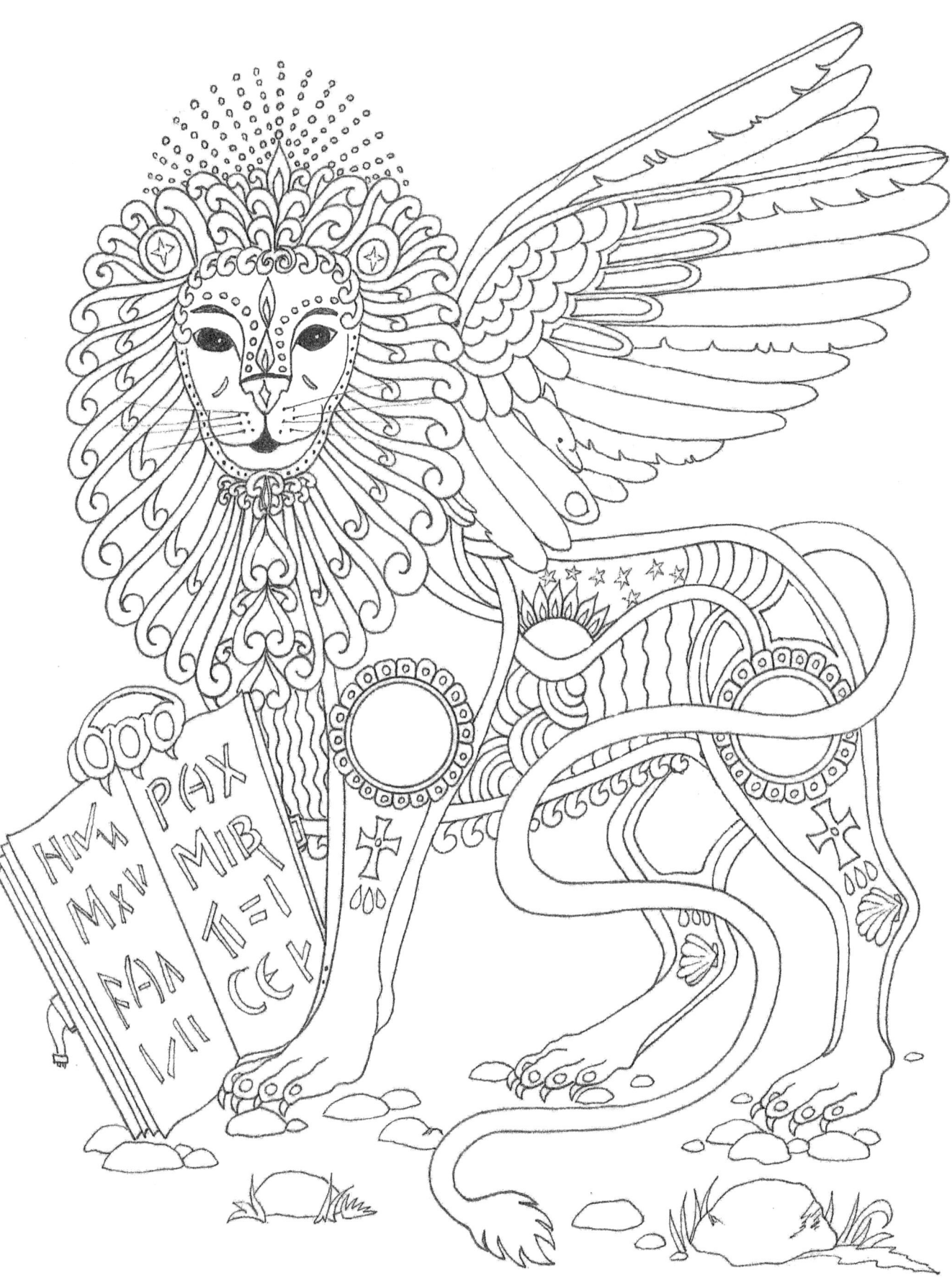

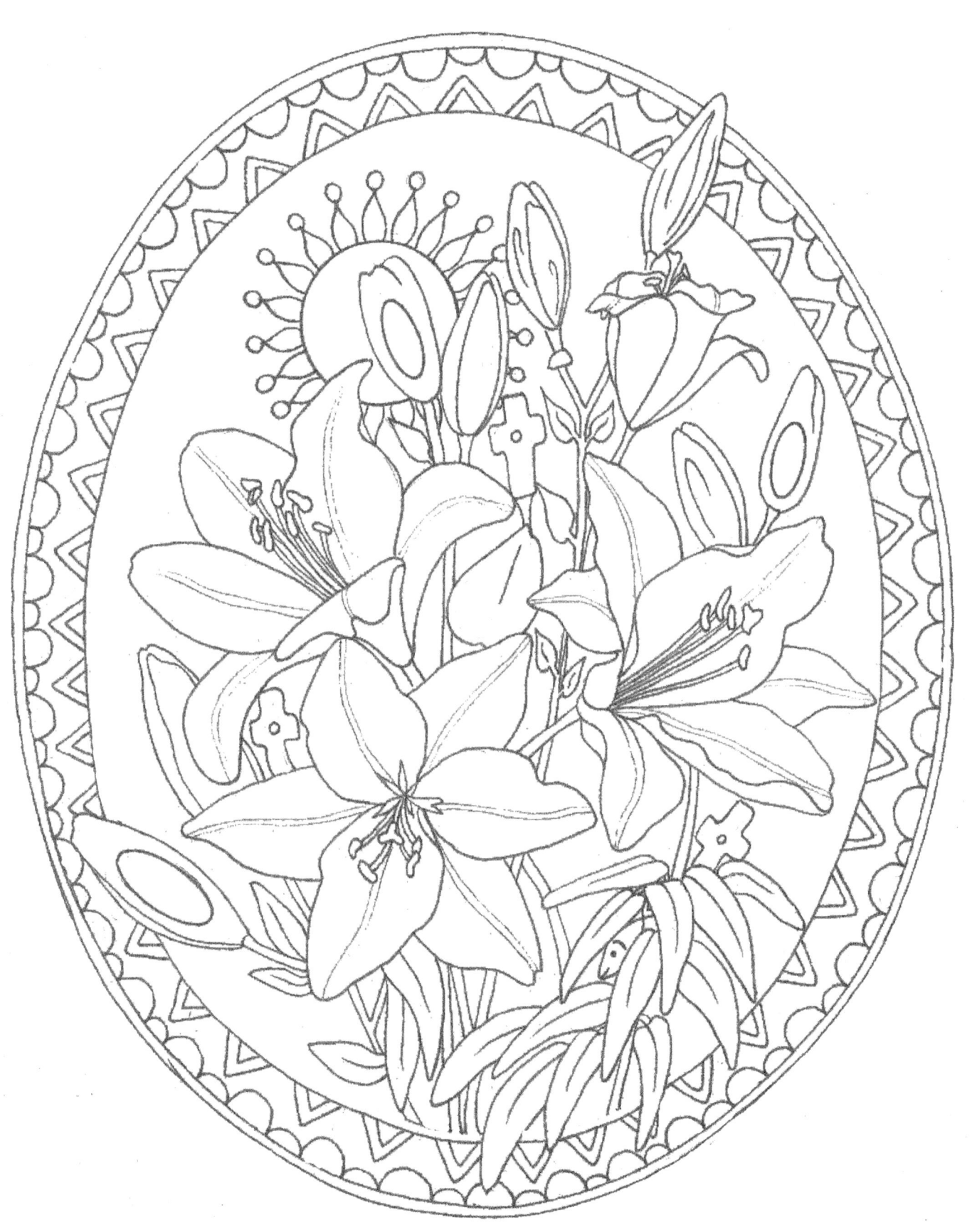

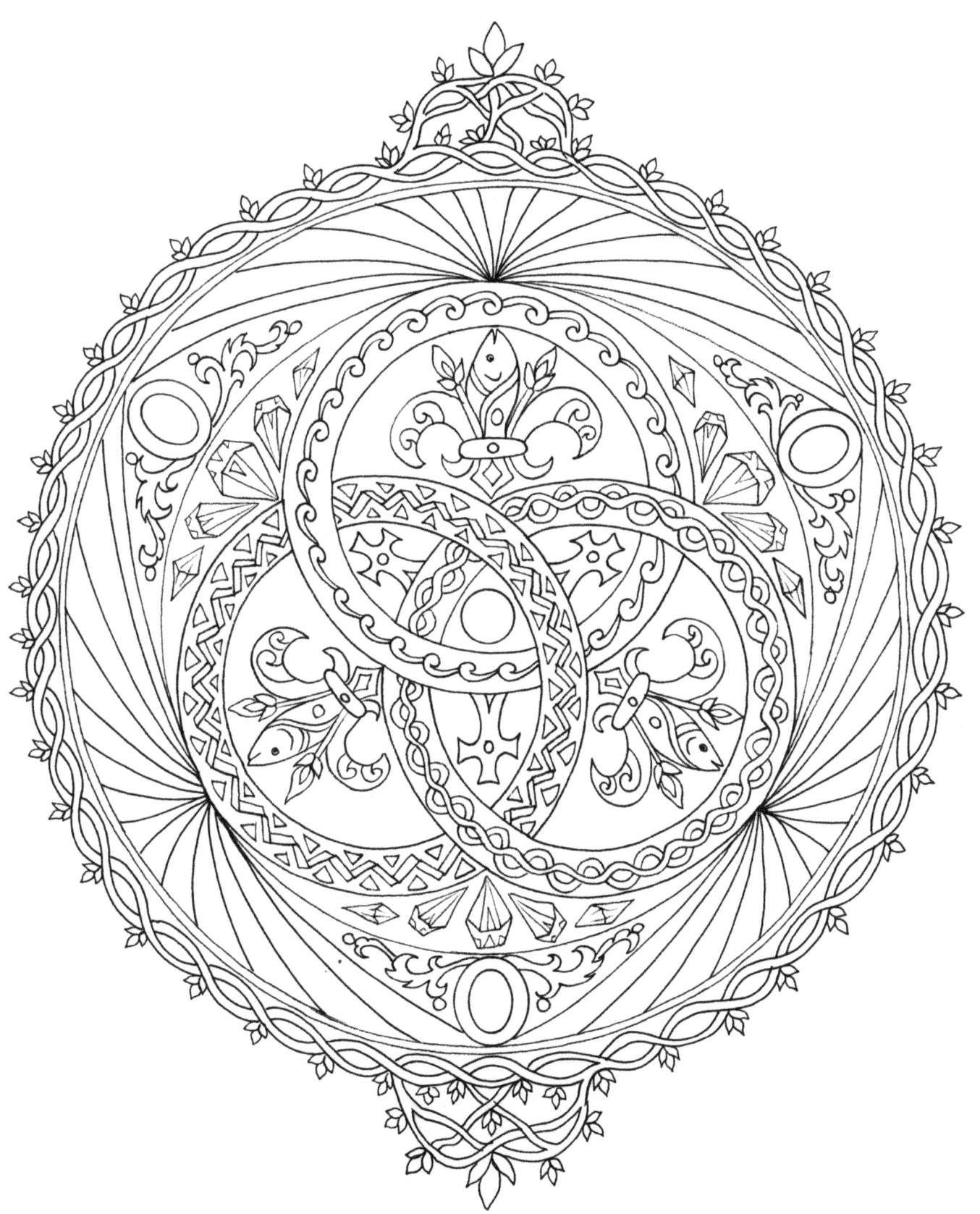

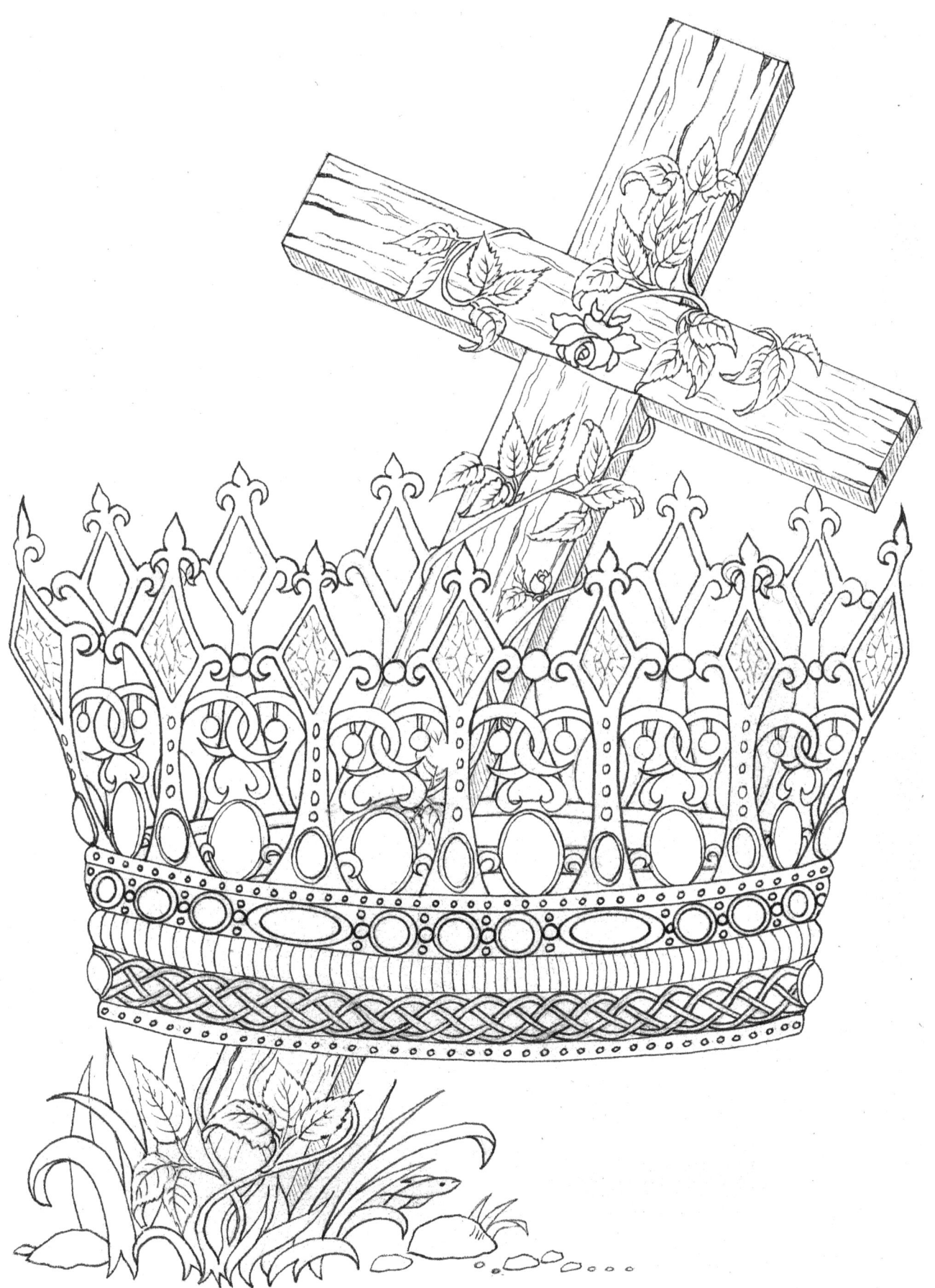

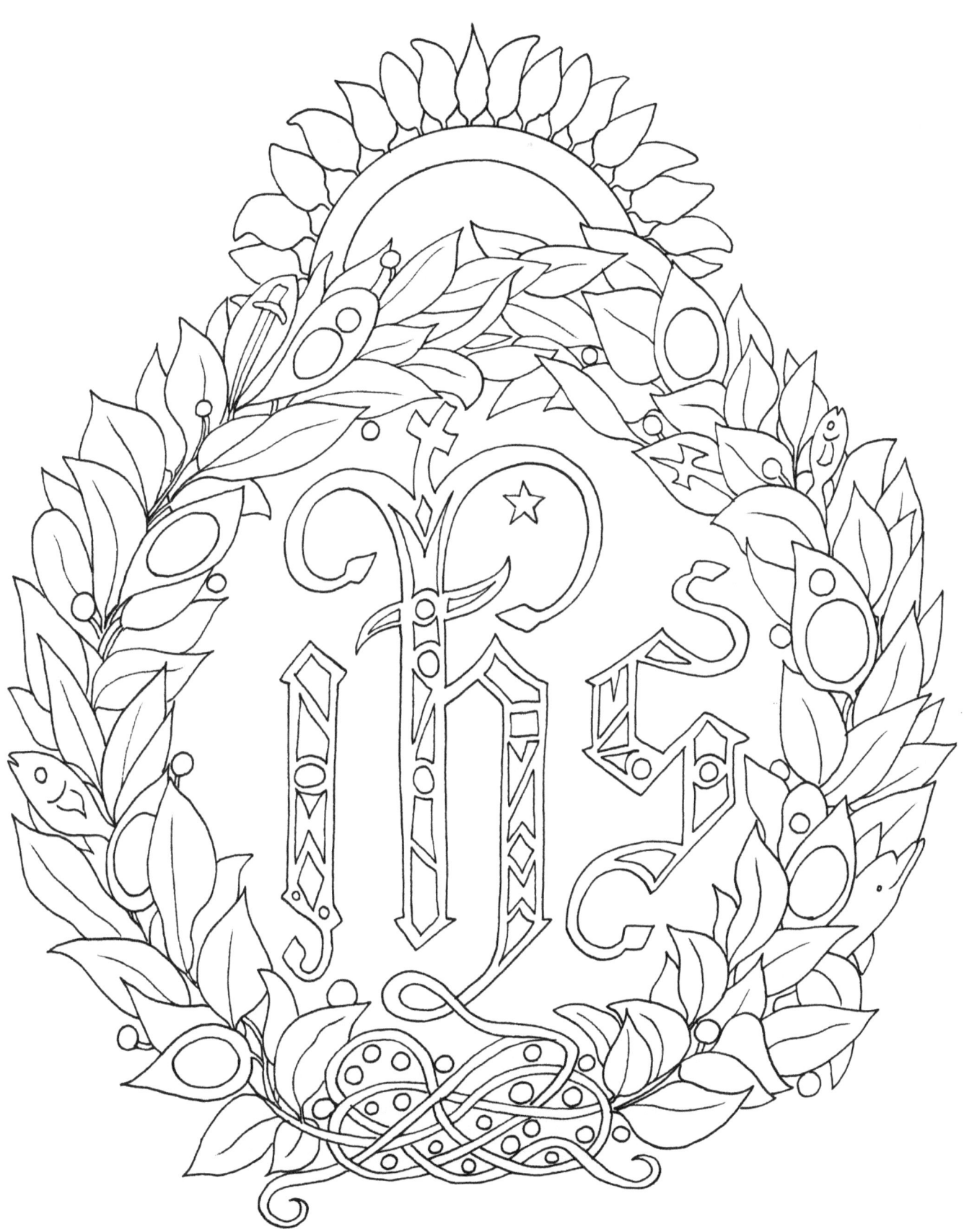

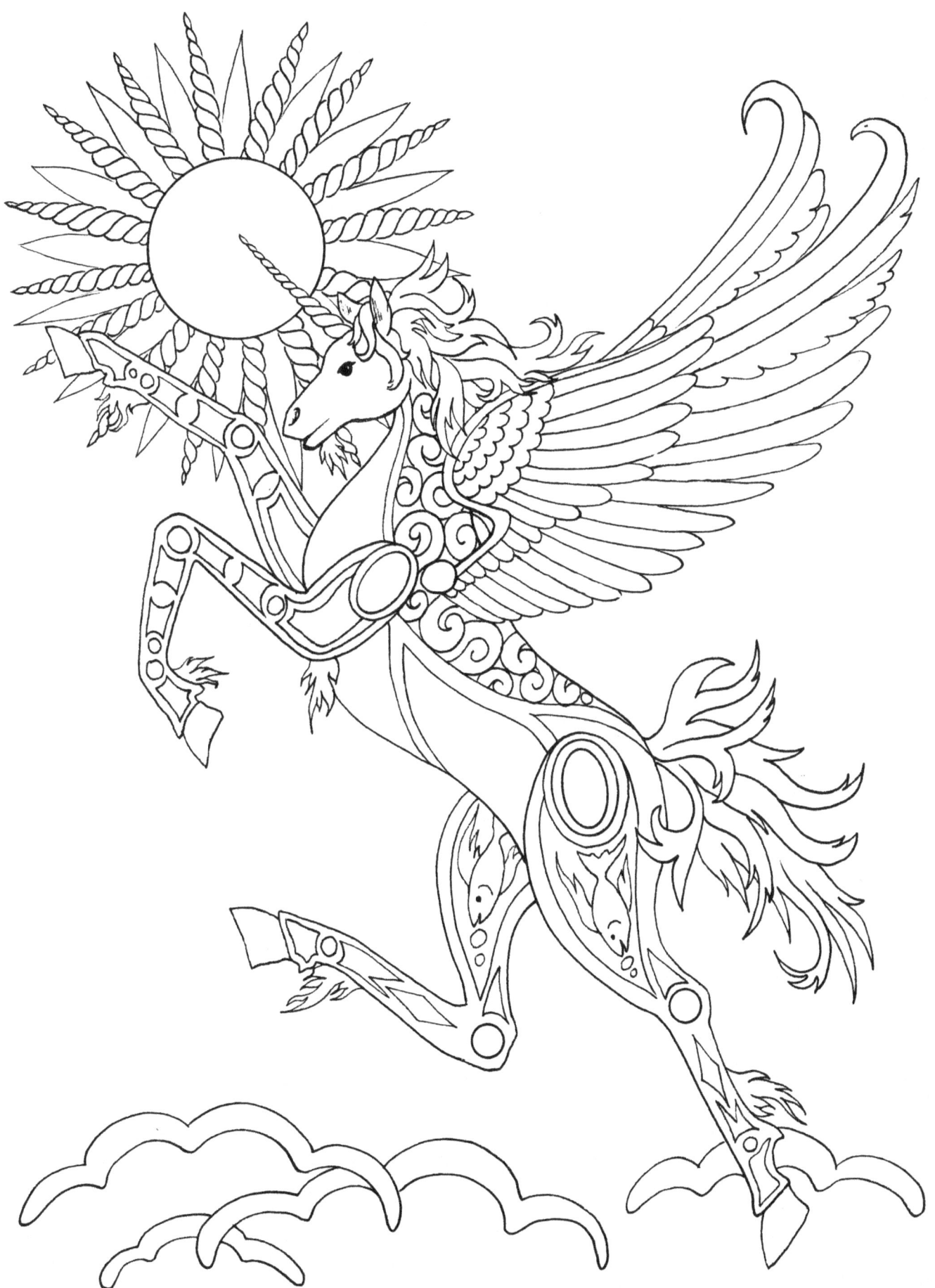

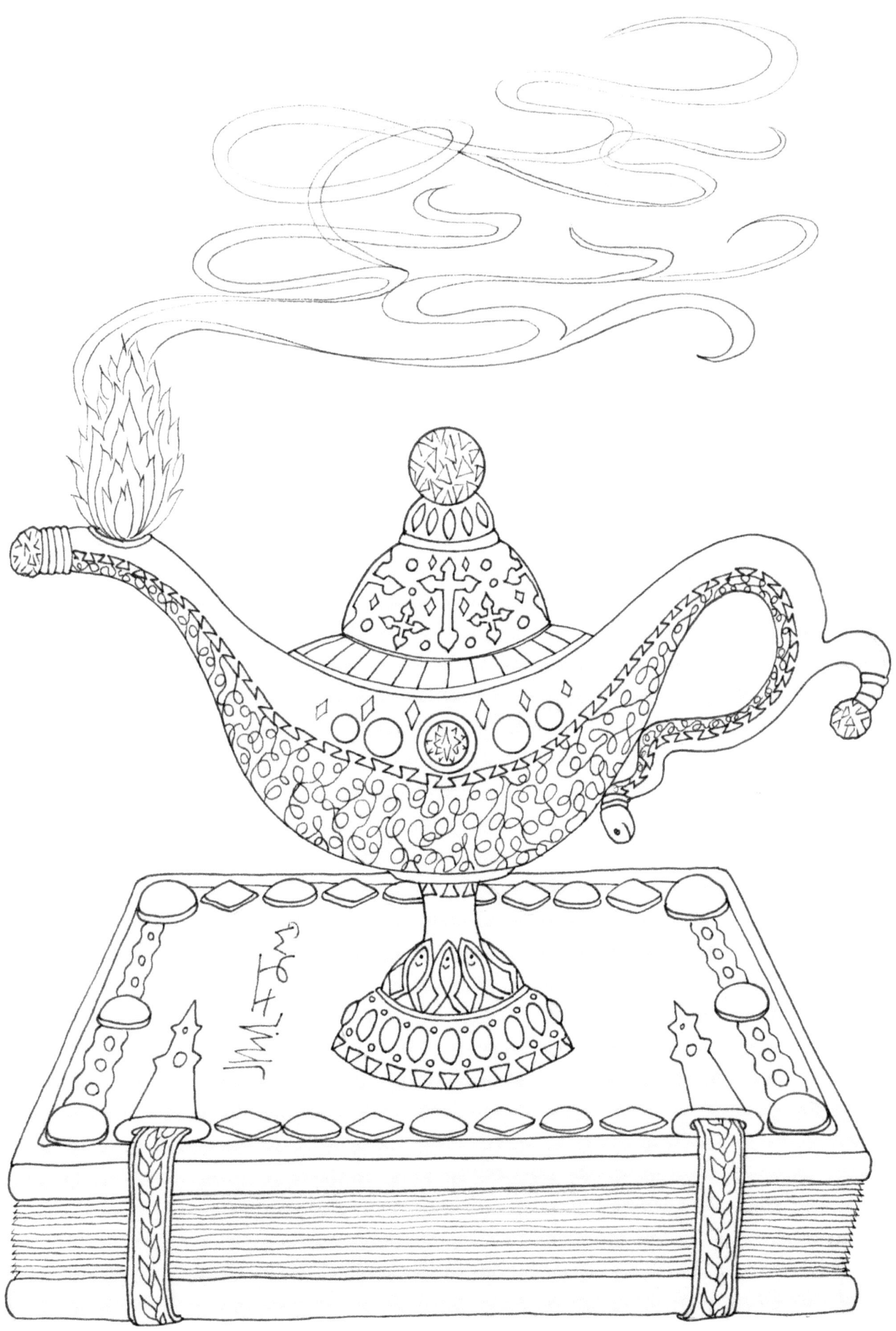

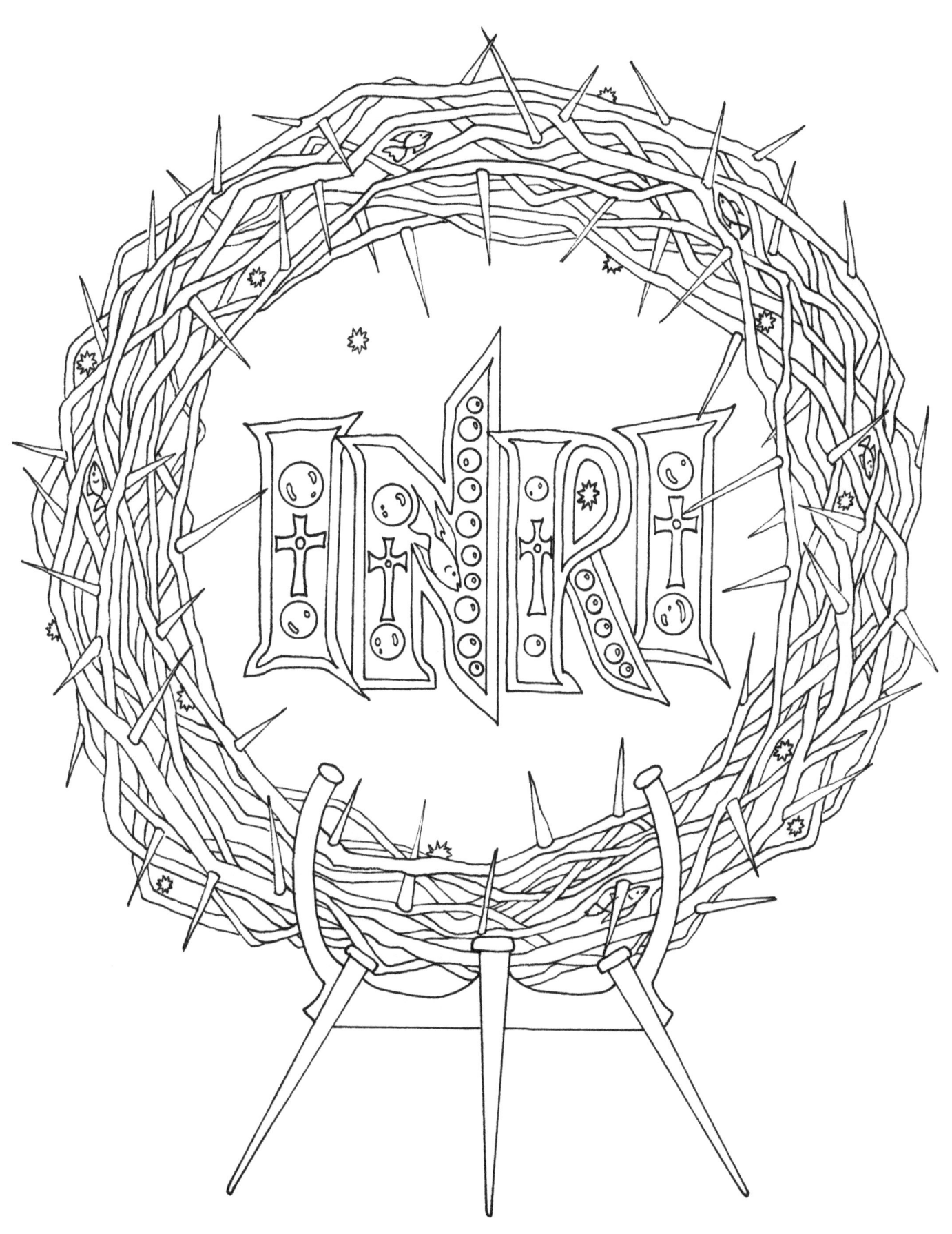

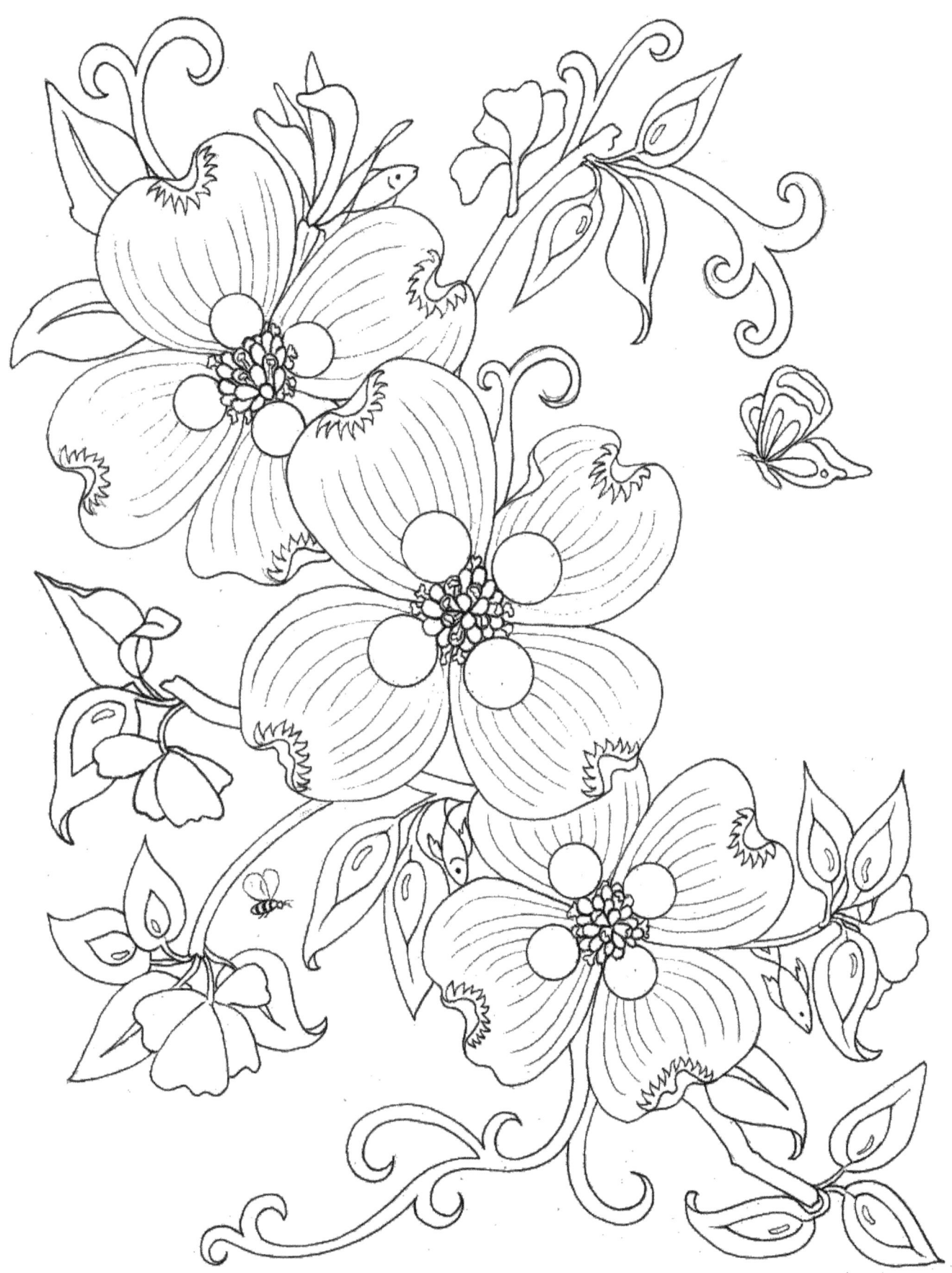

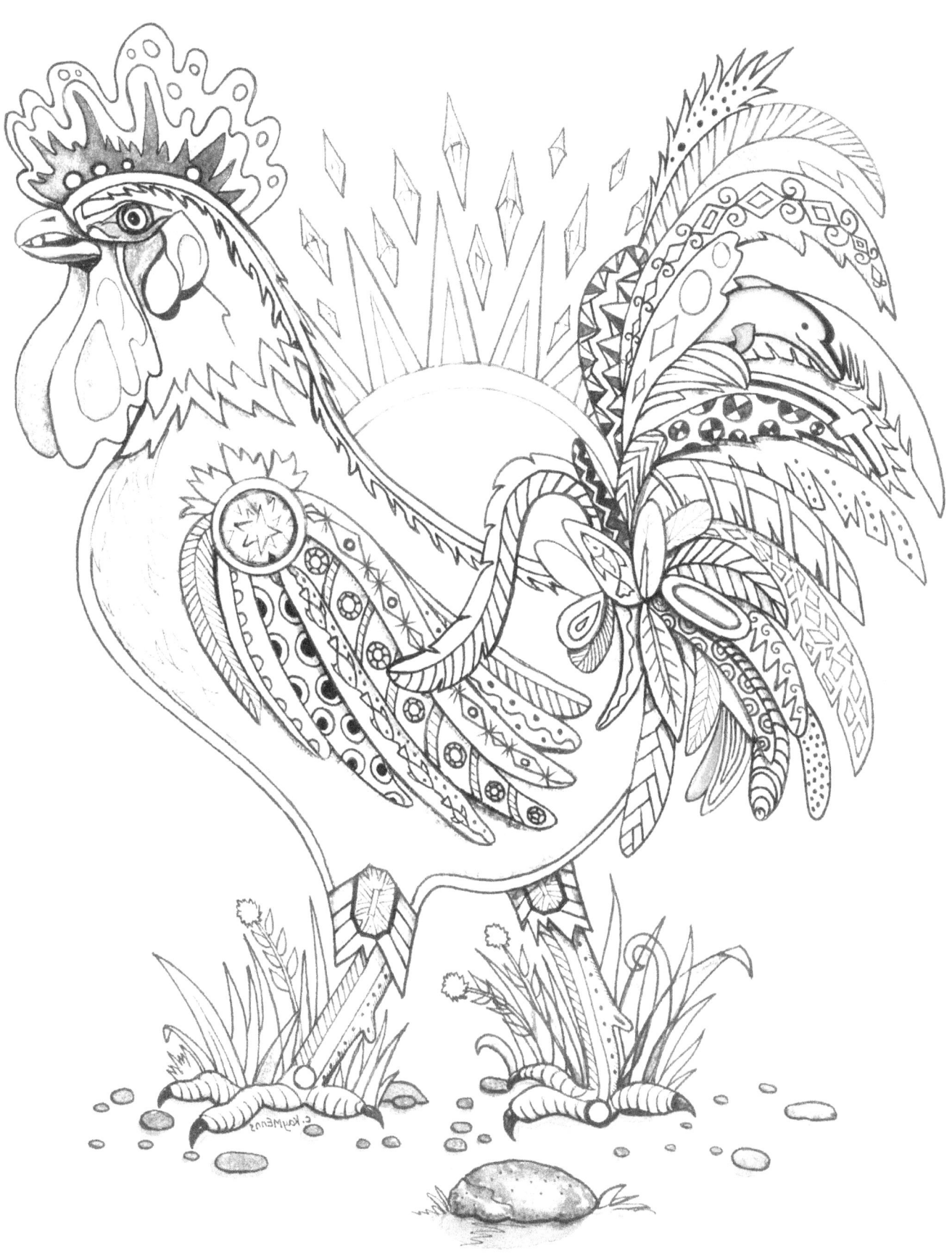

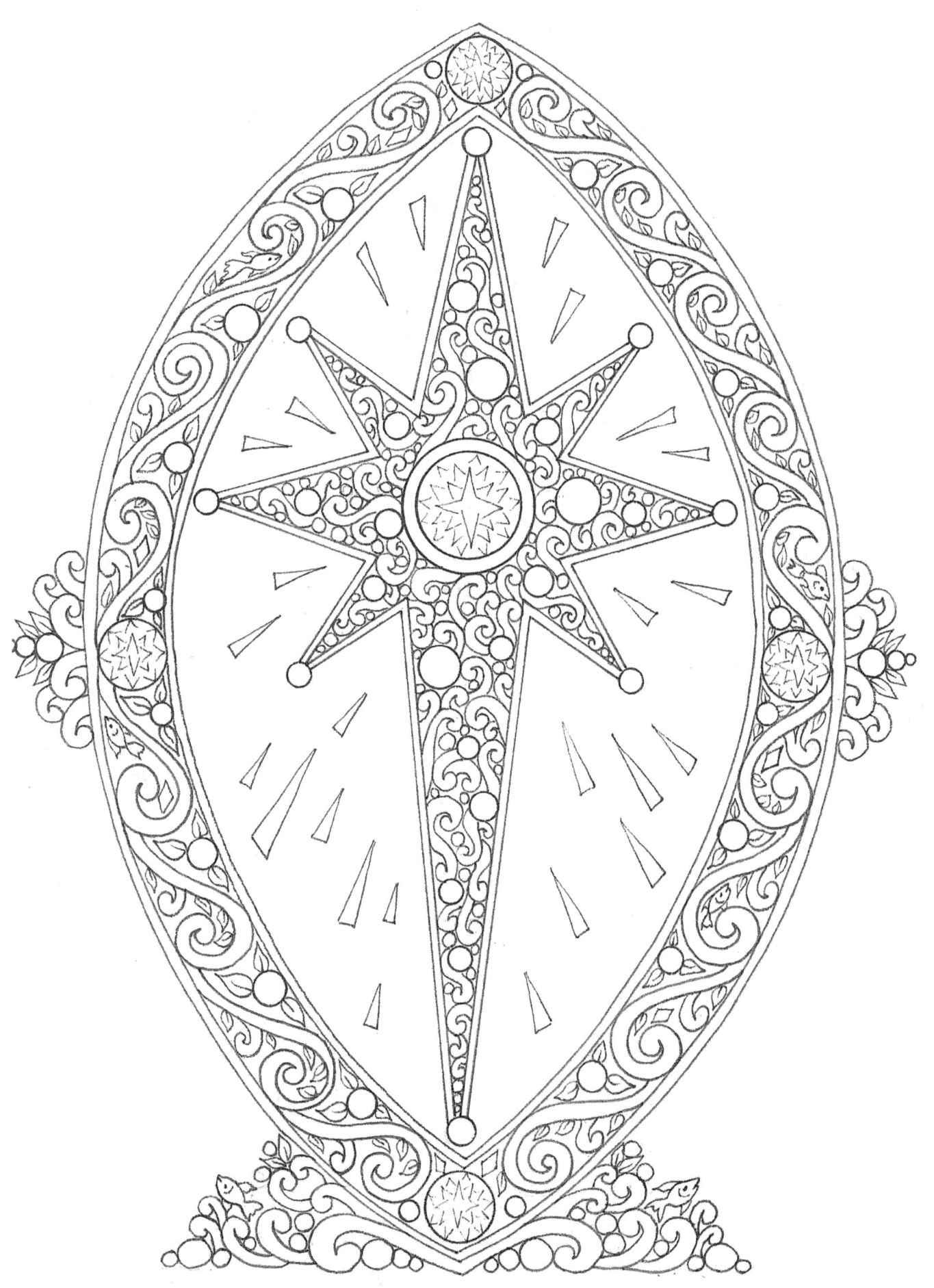

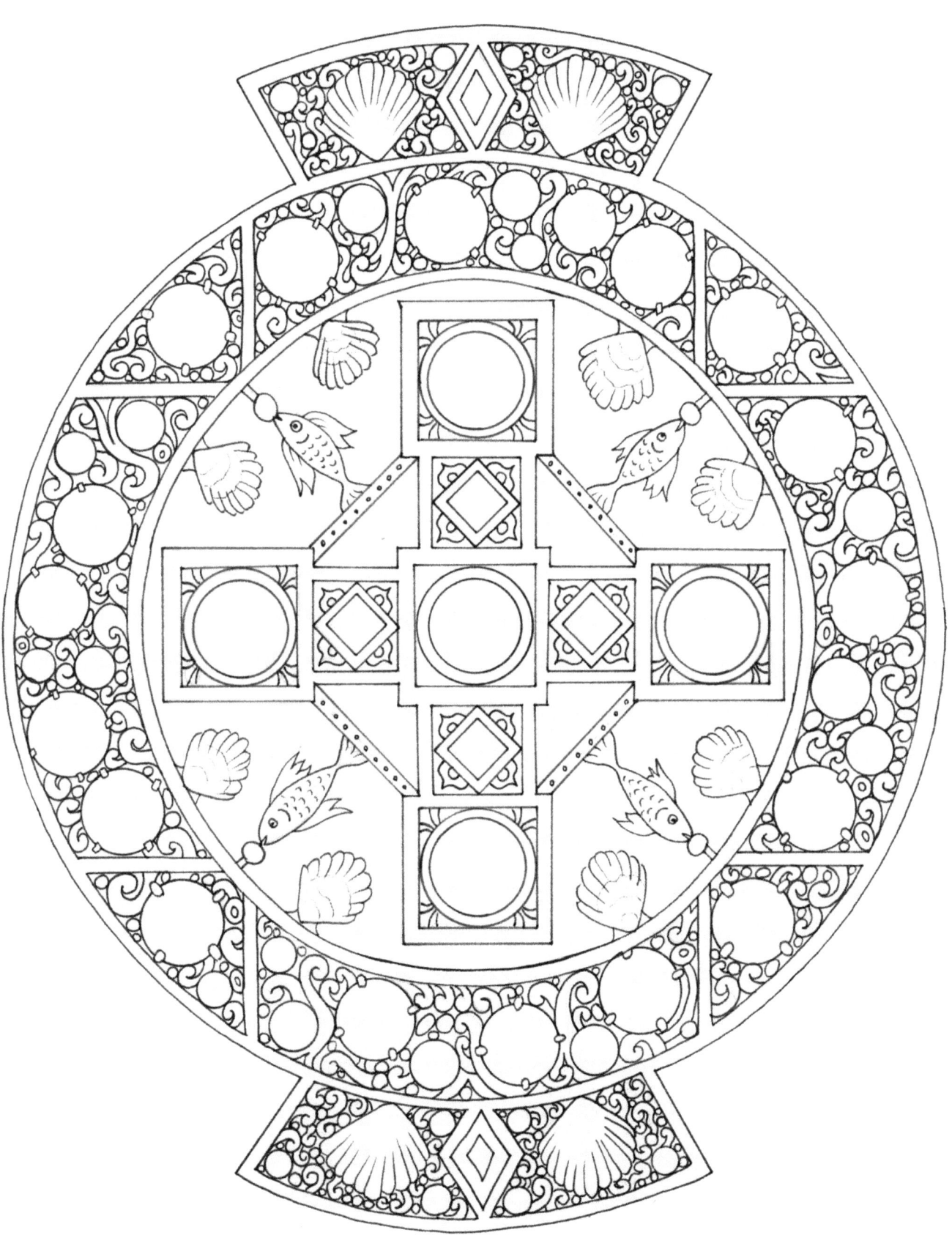

I

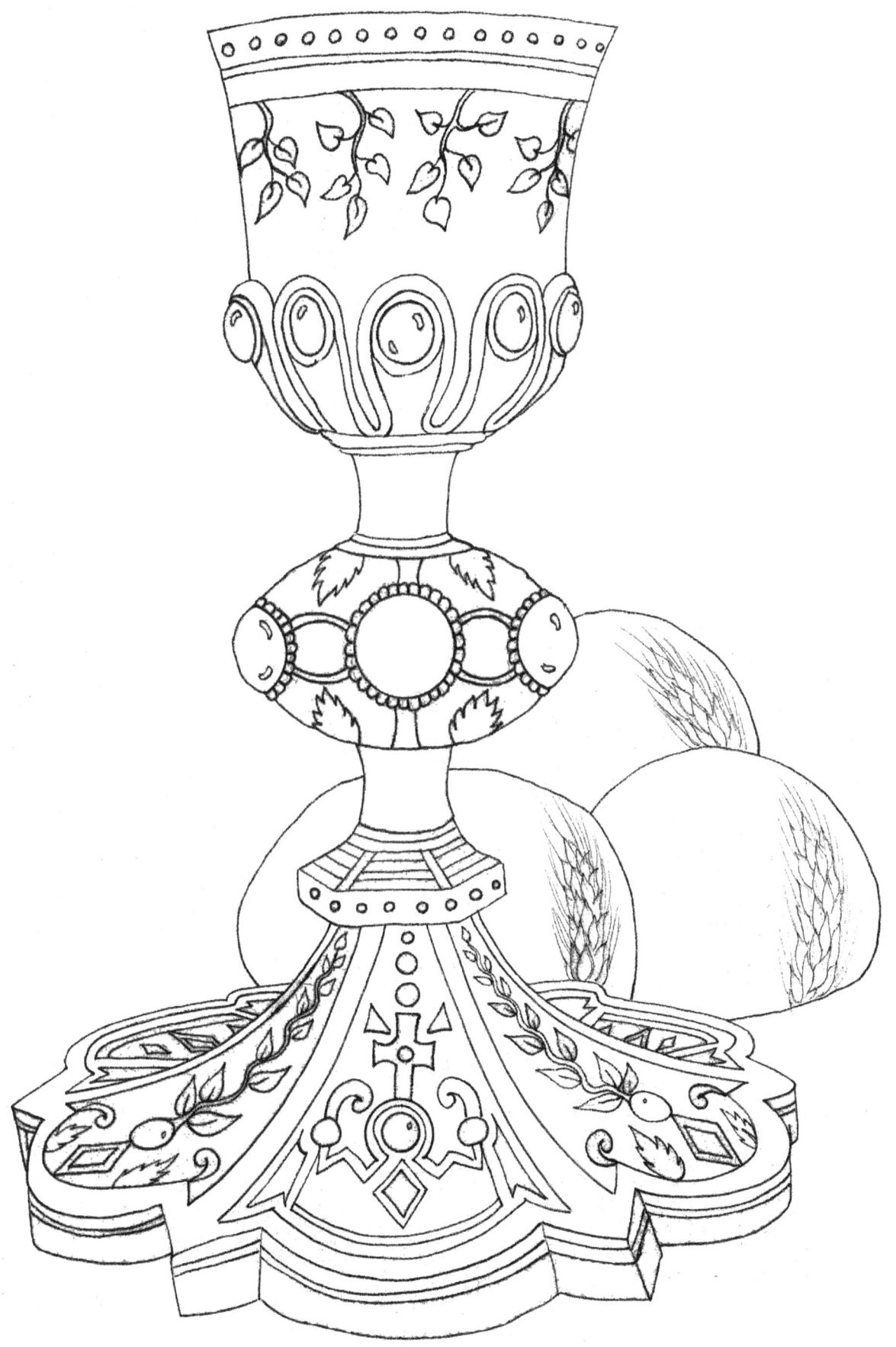

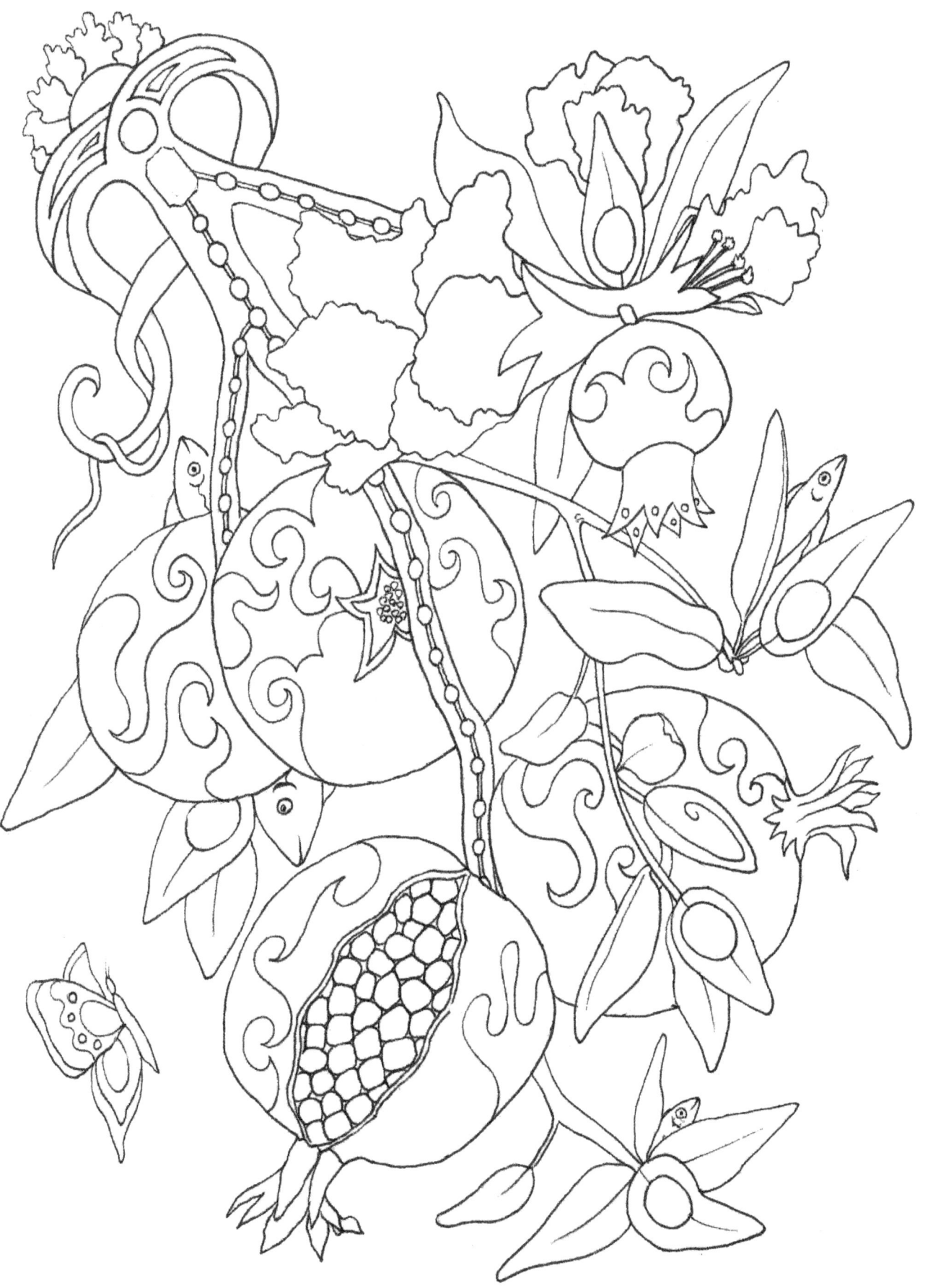

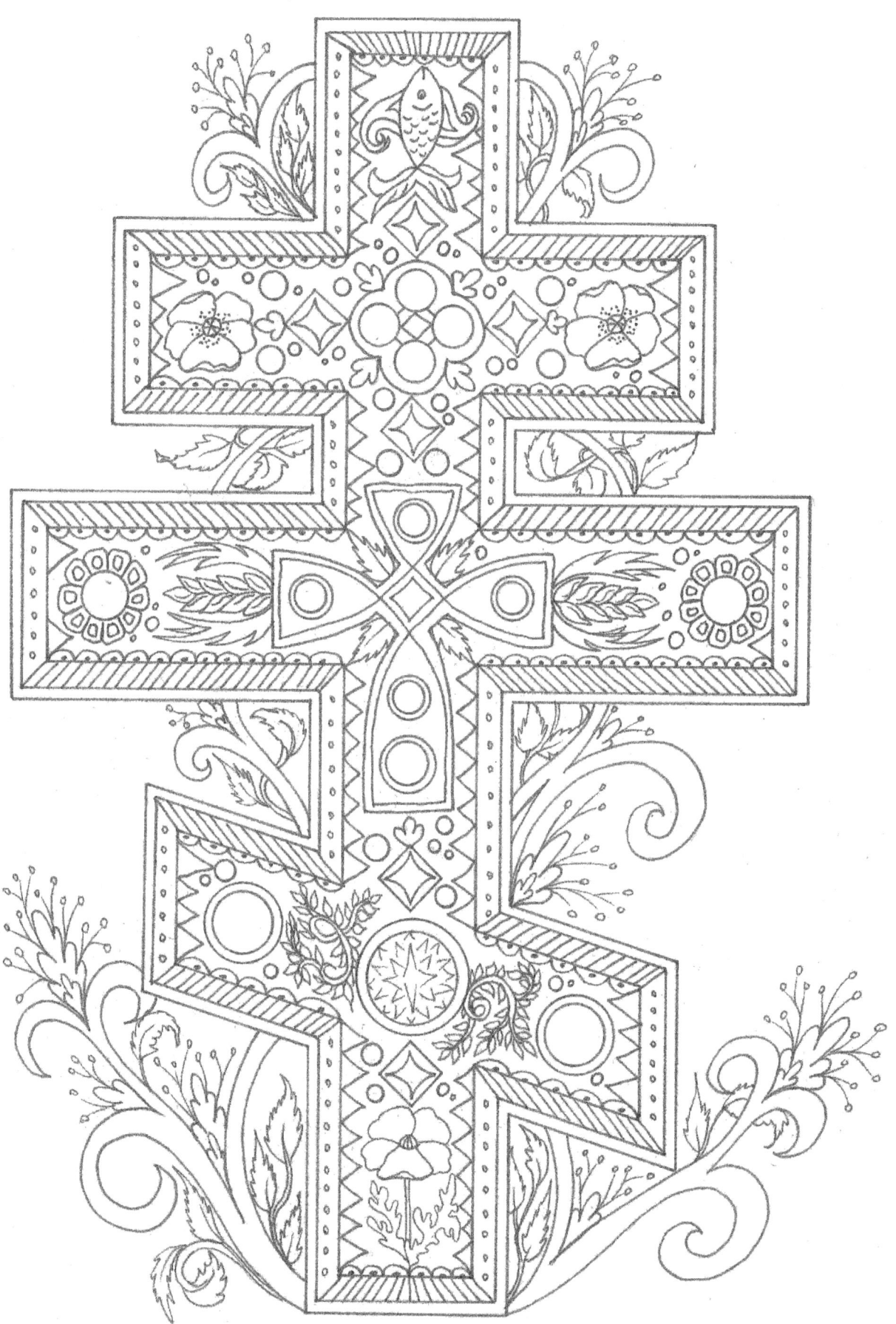

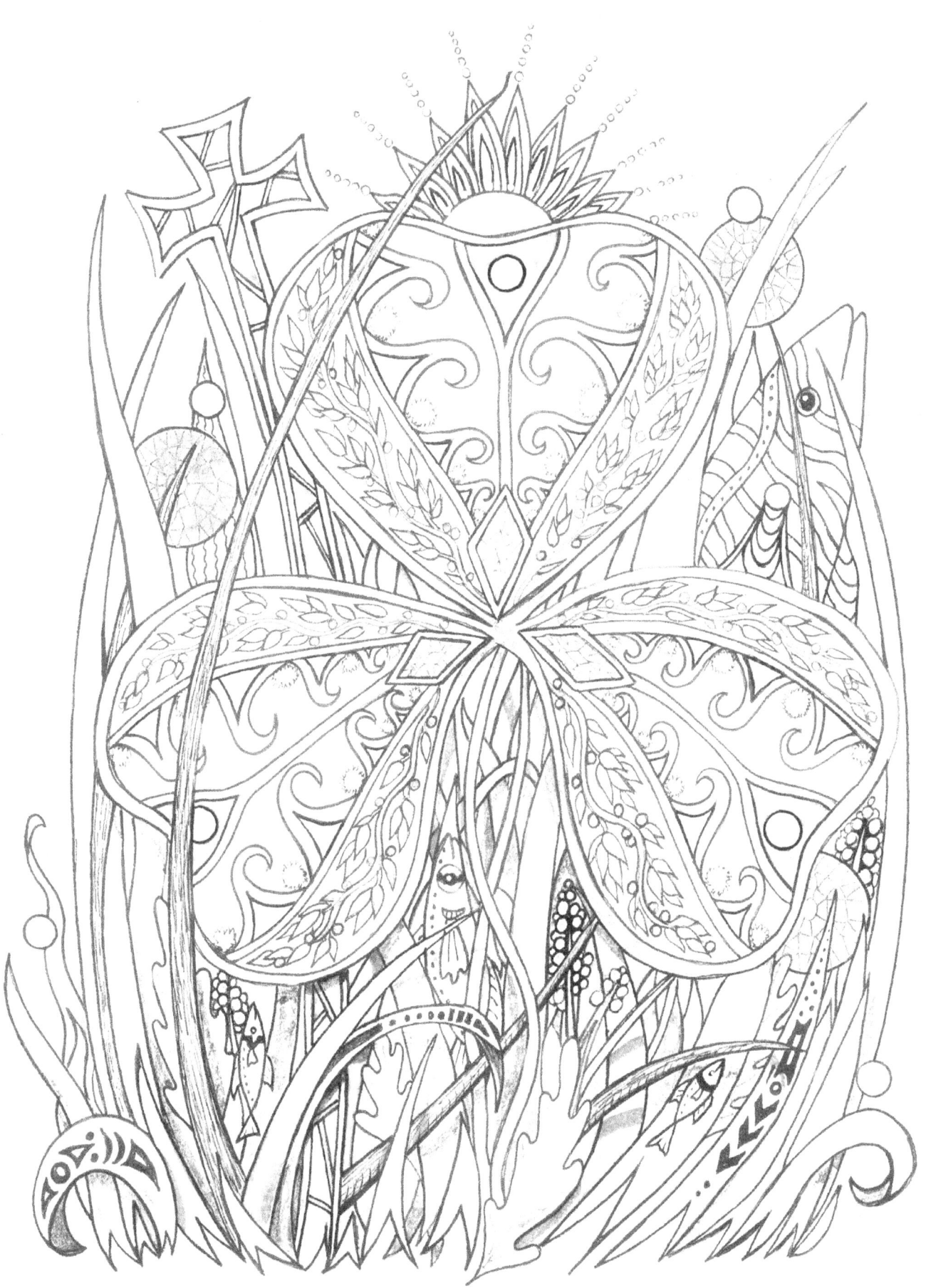

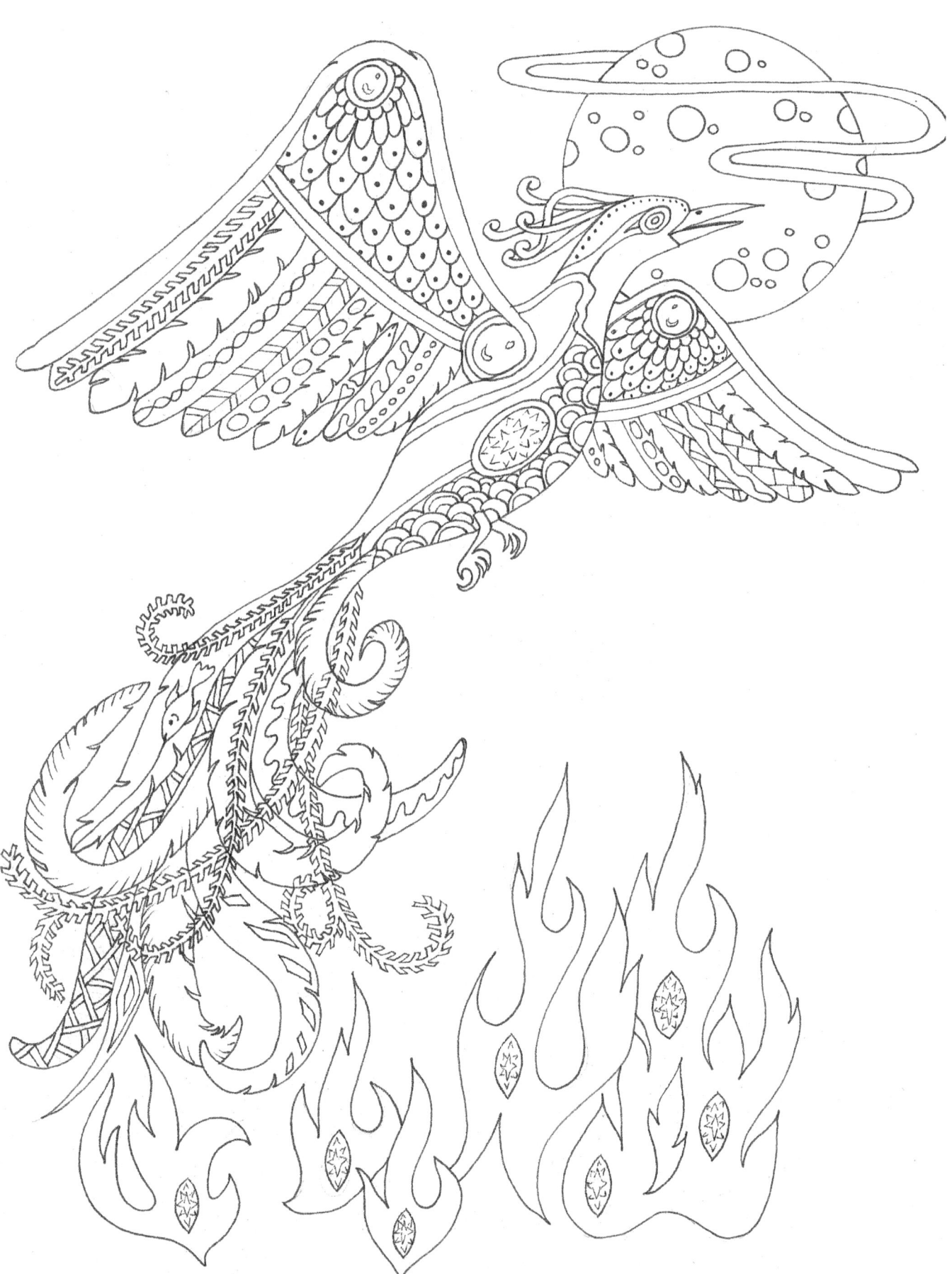

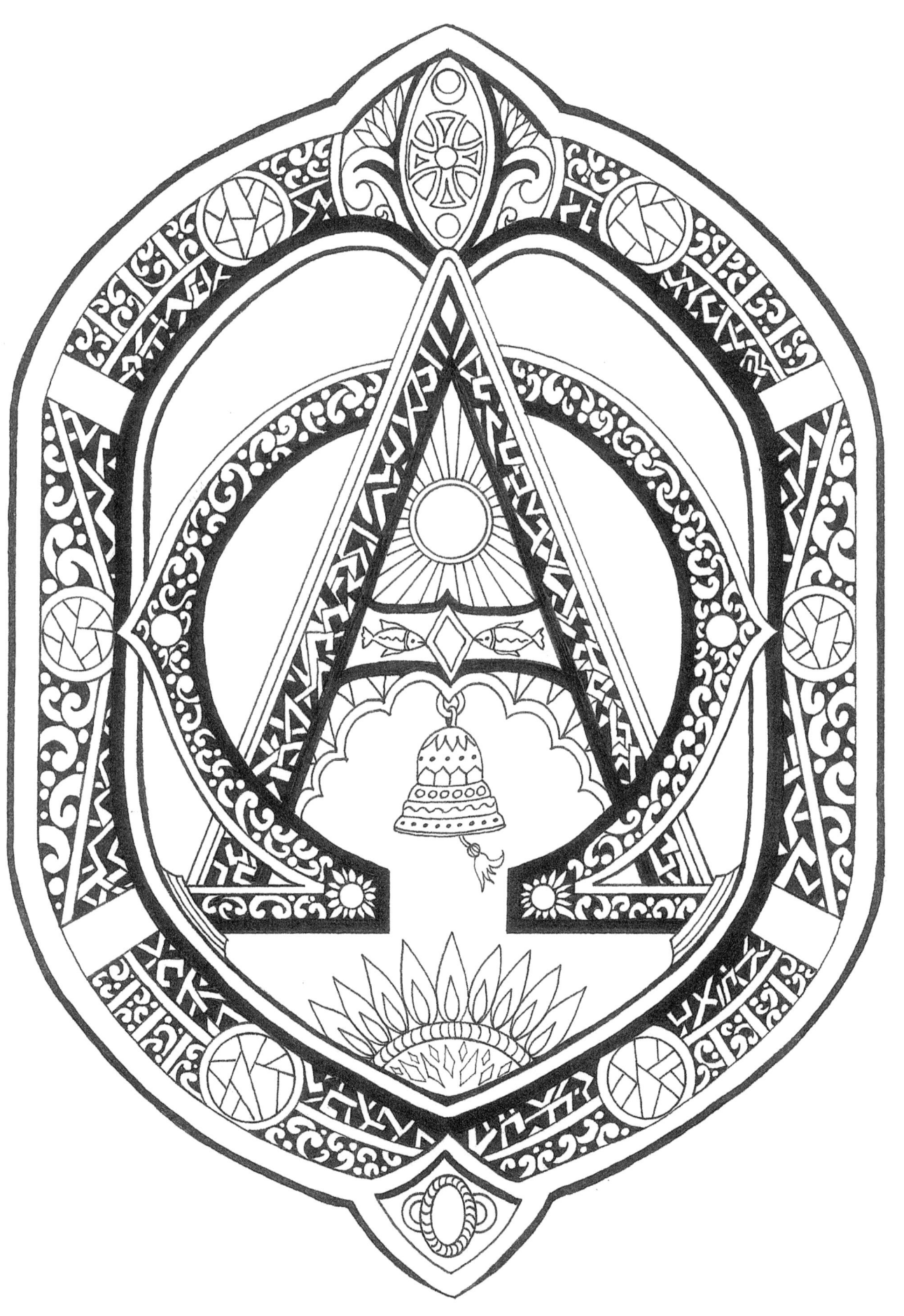

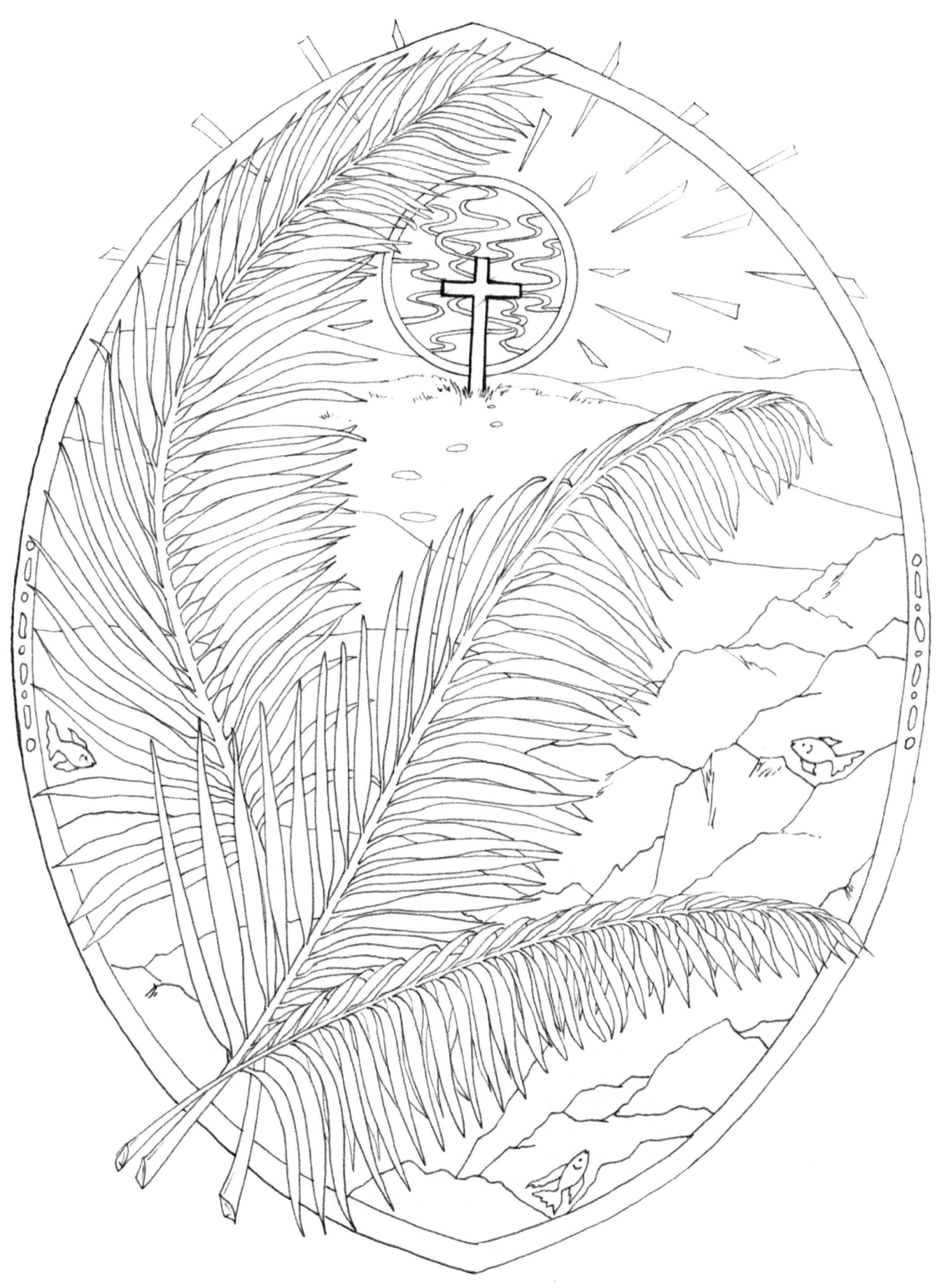

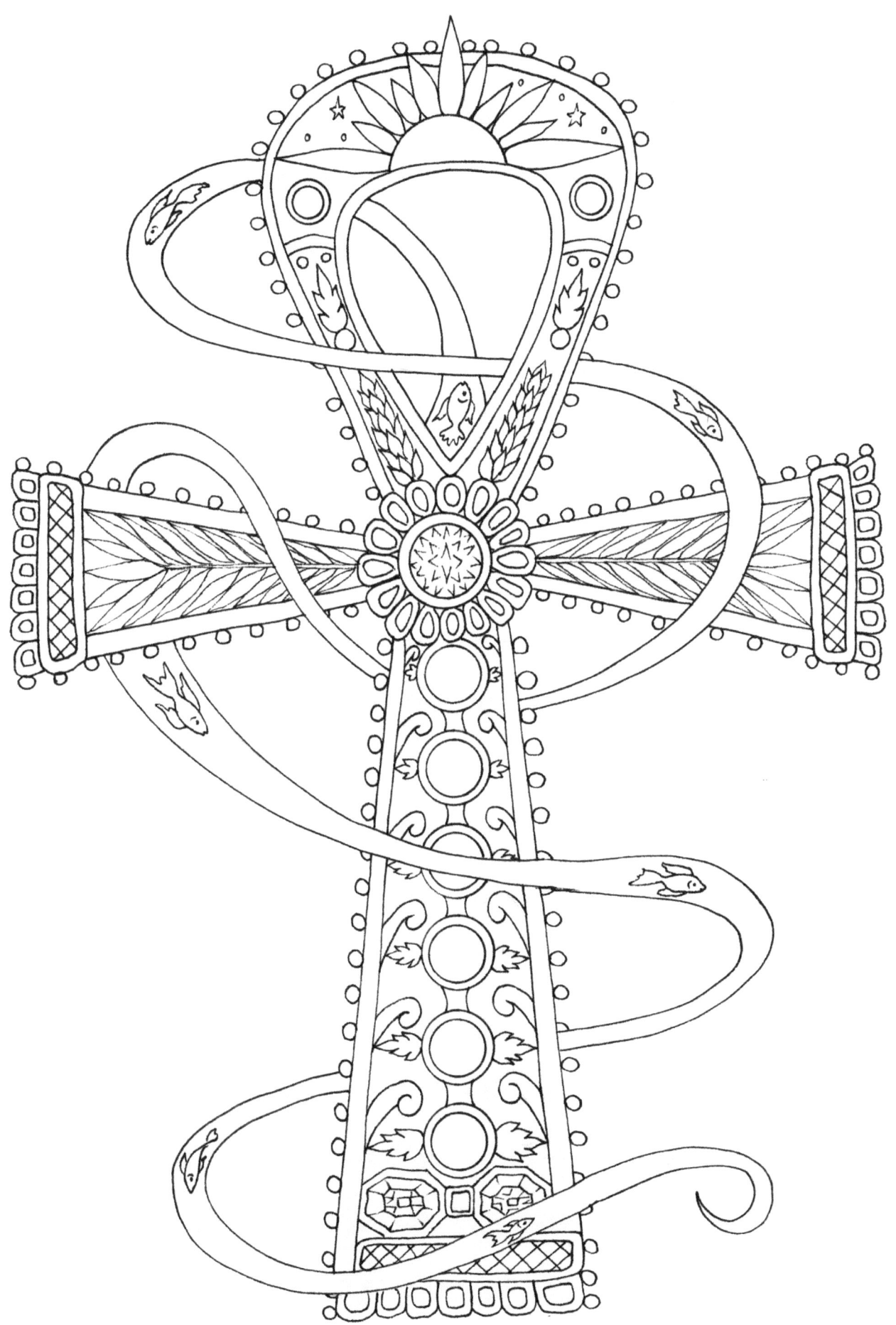

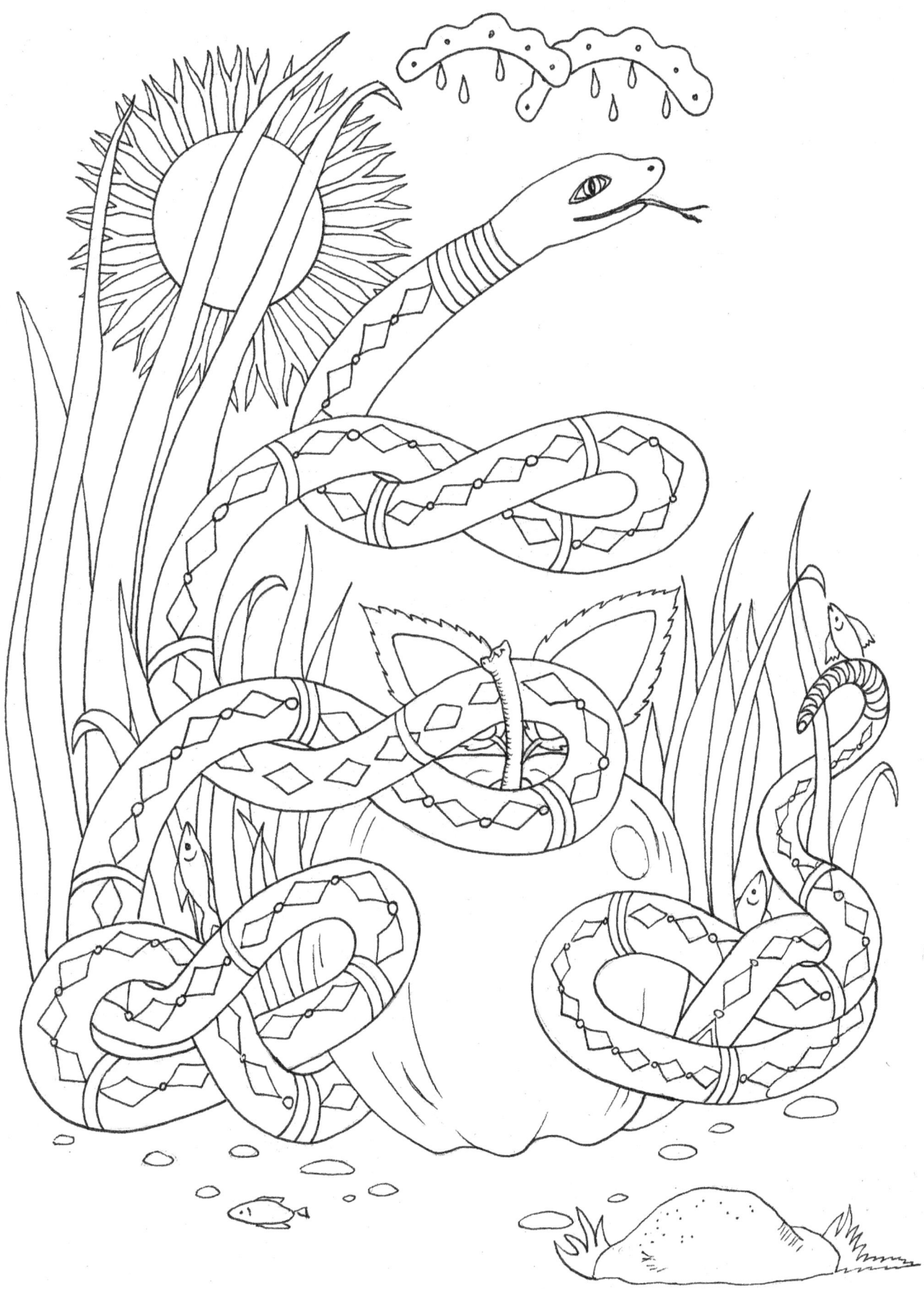

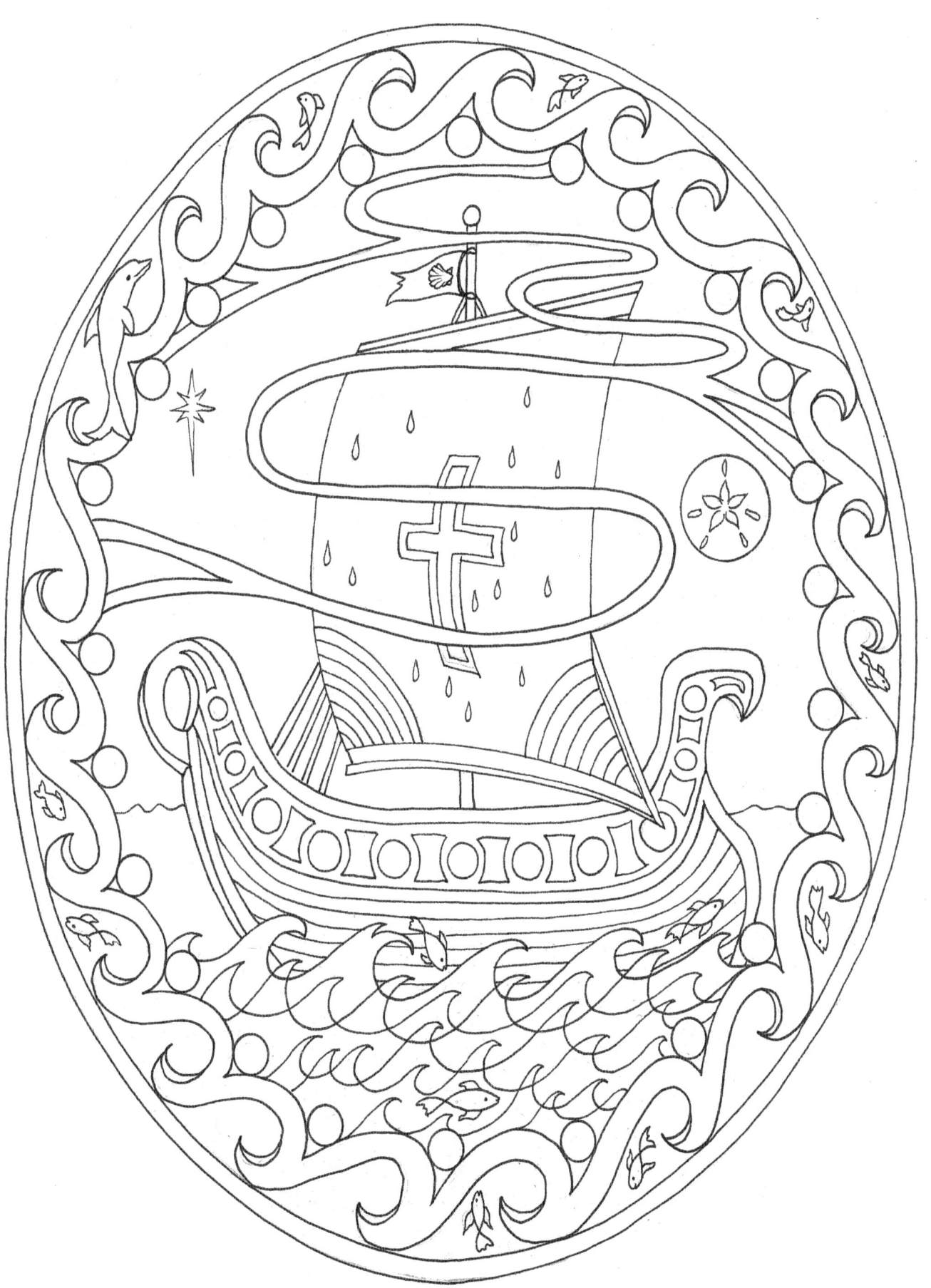

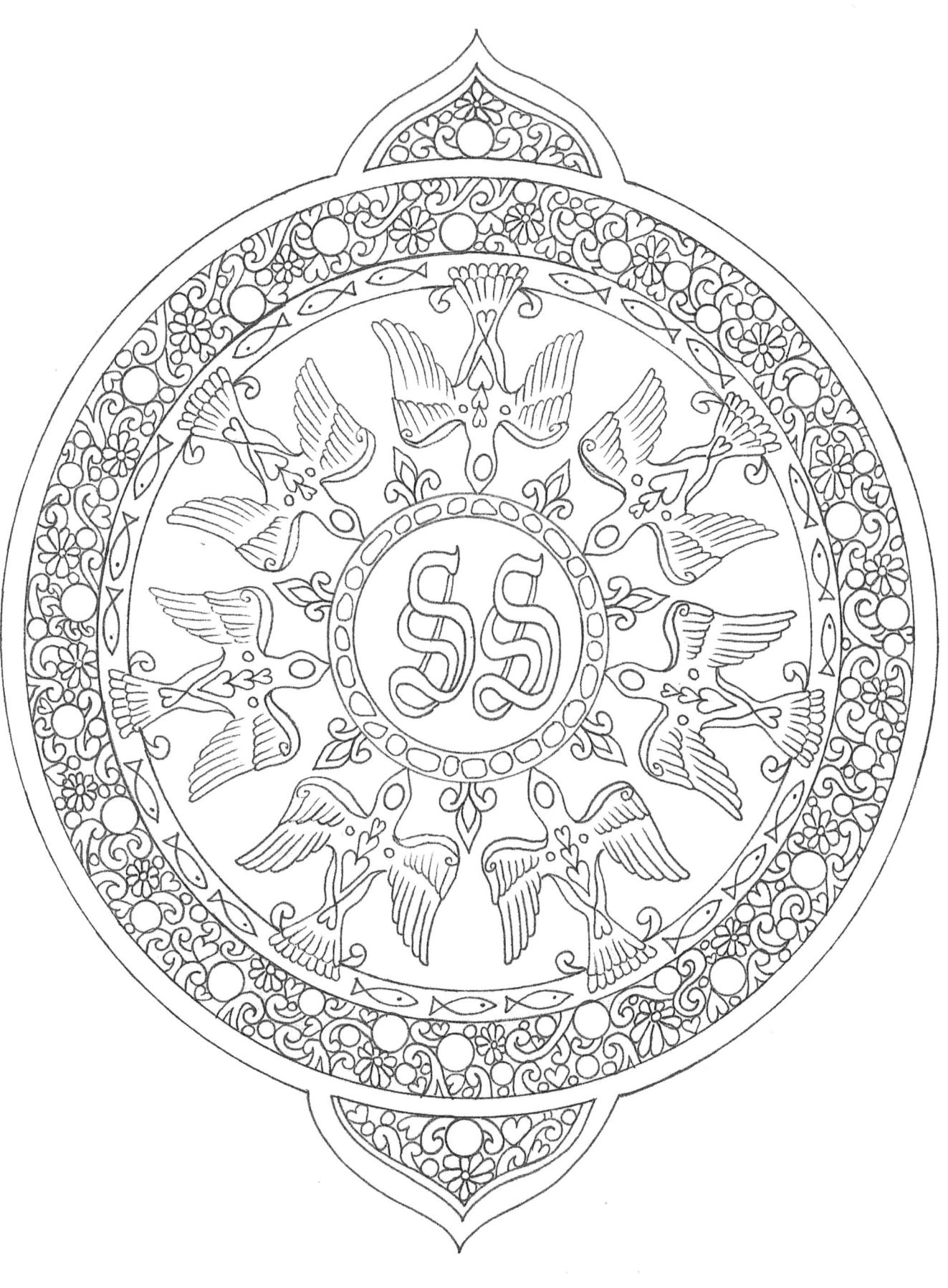

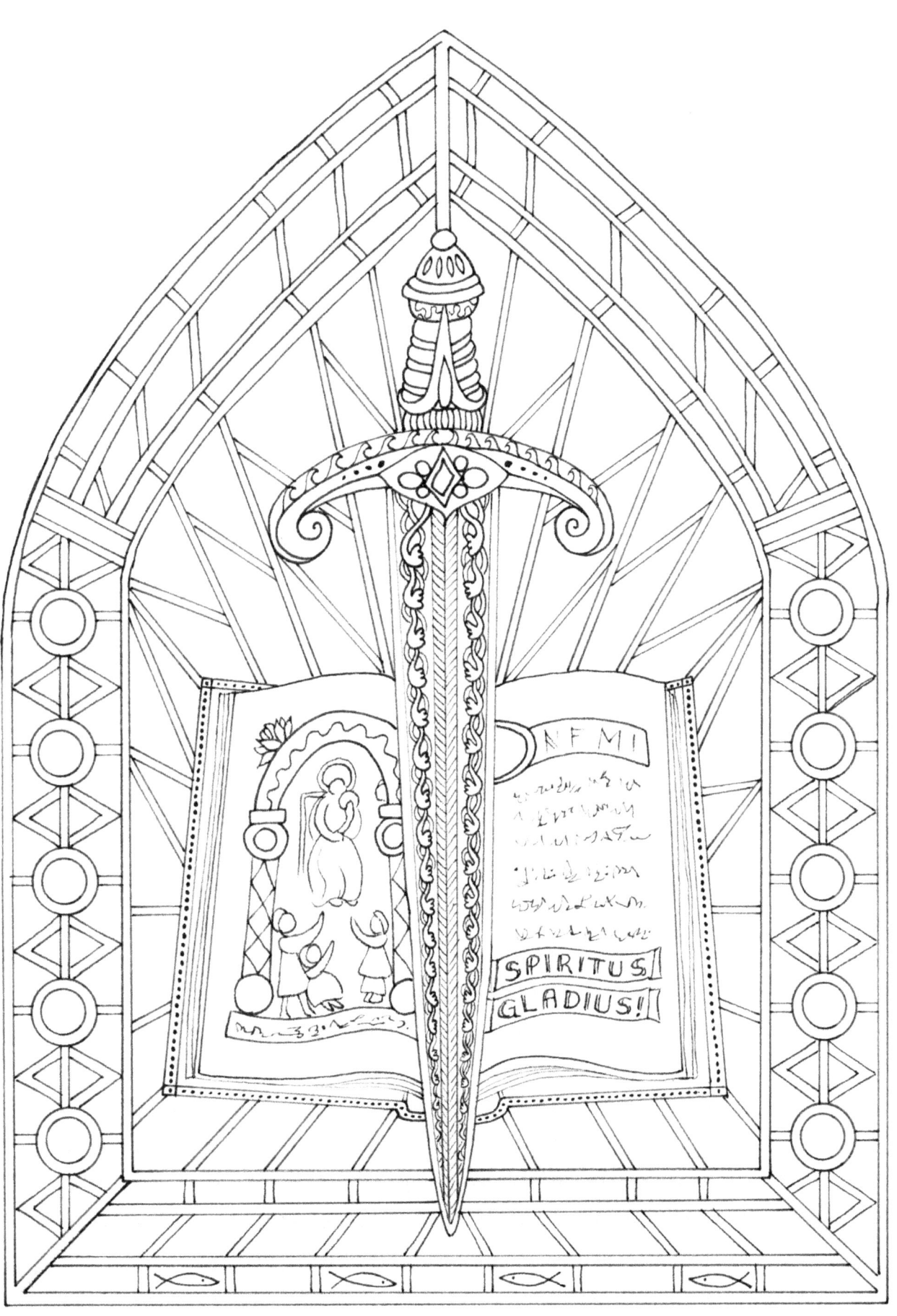

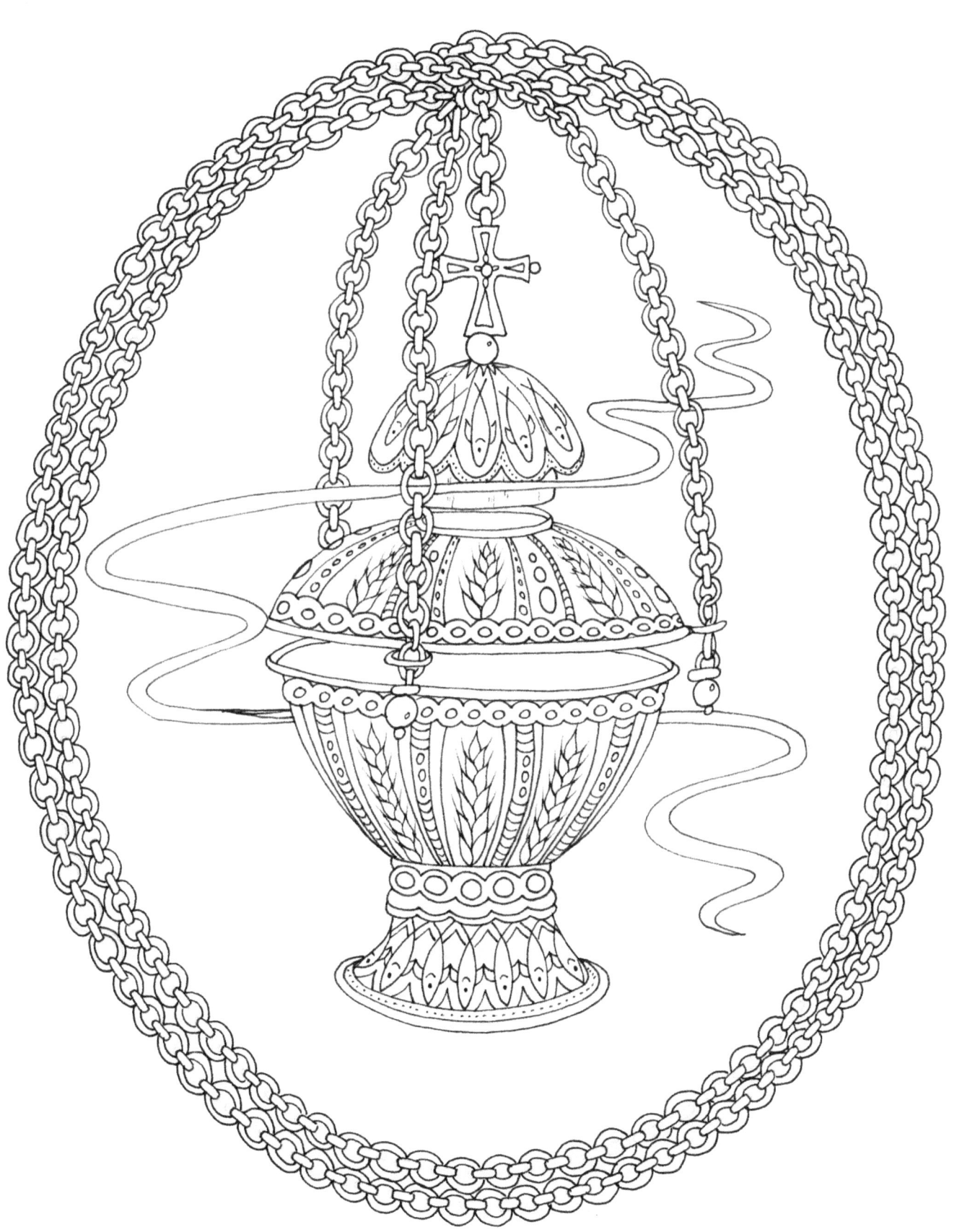

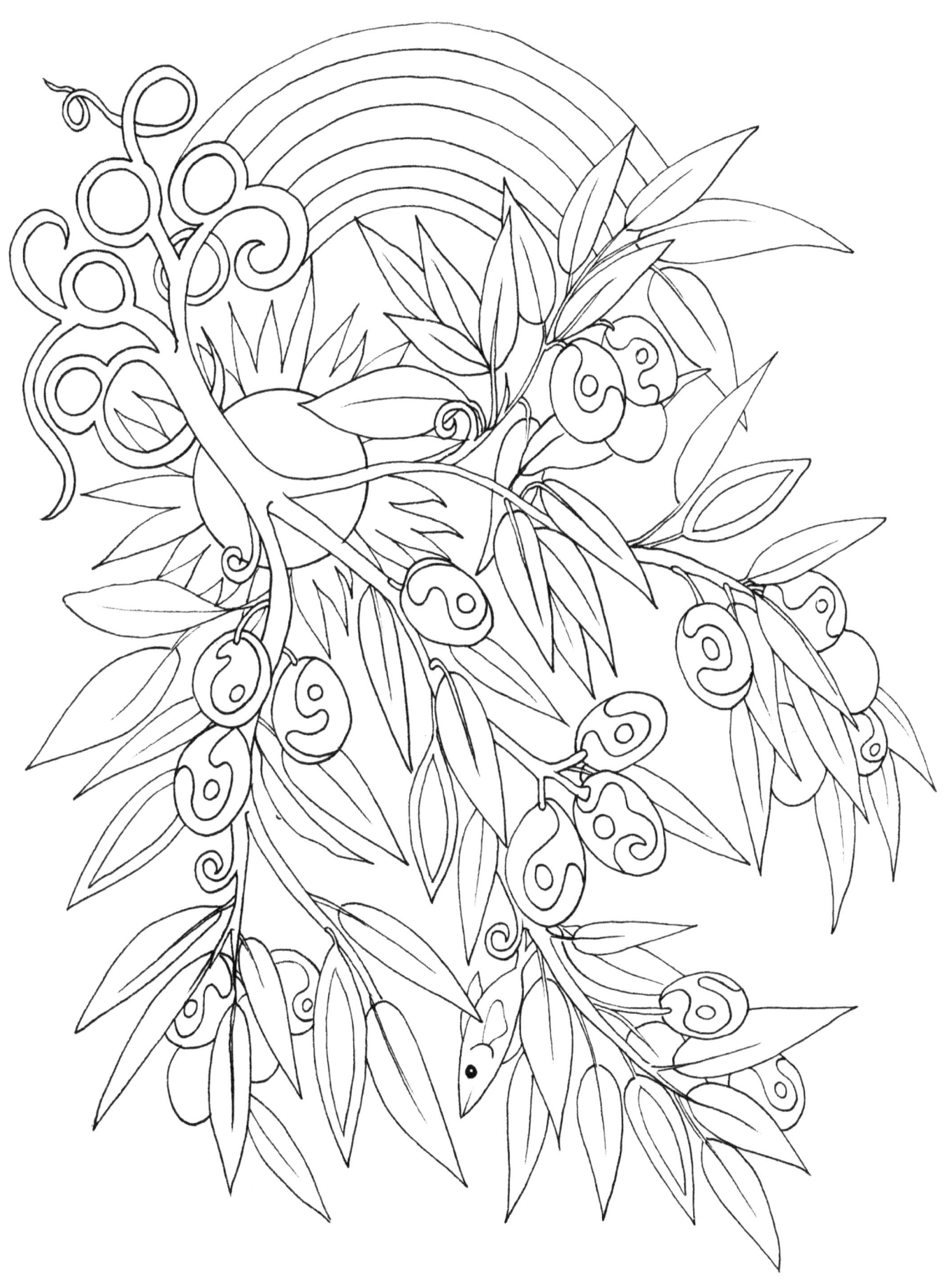

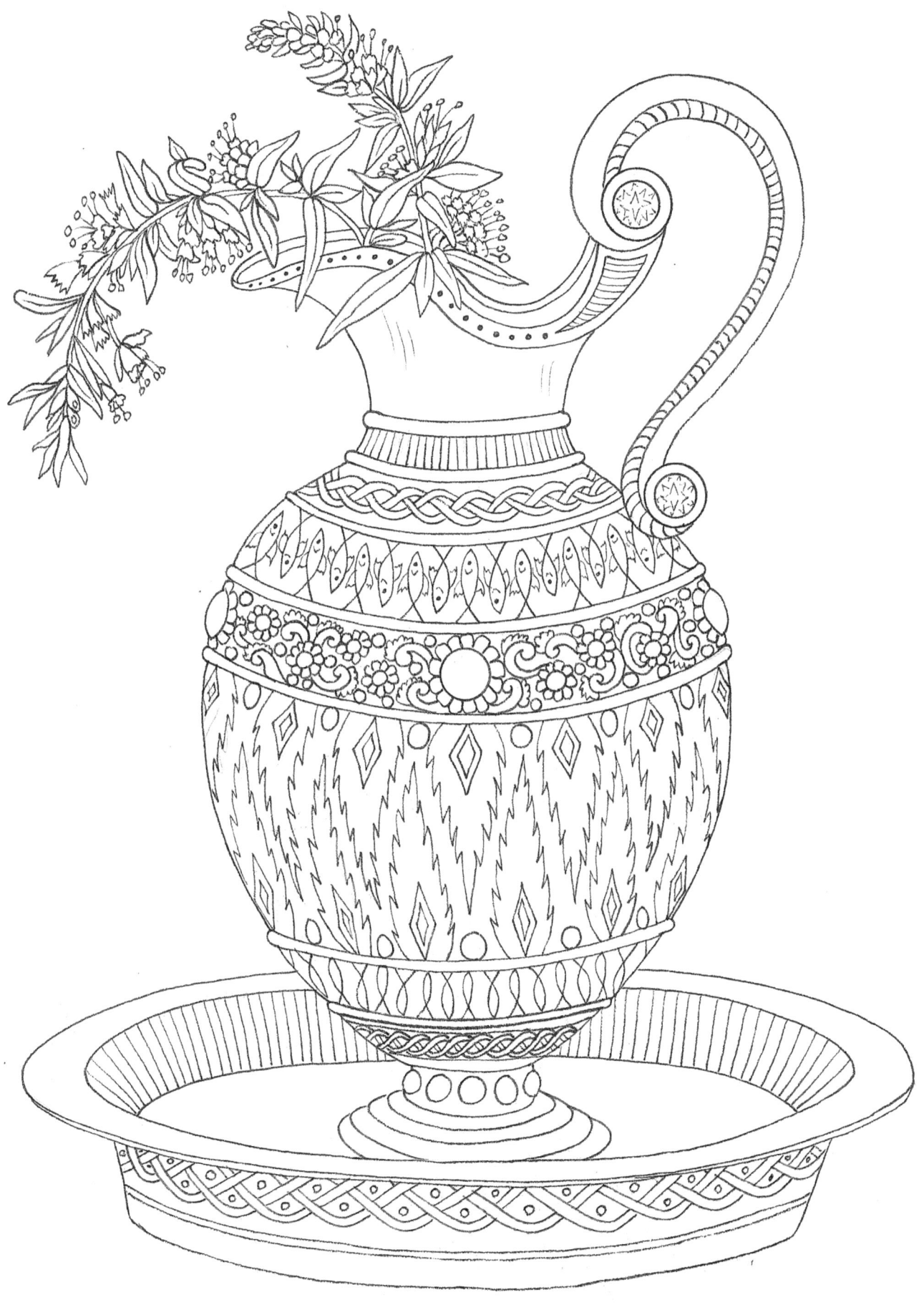

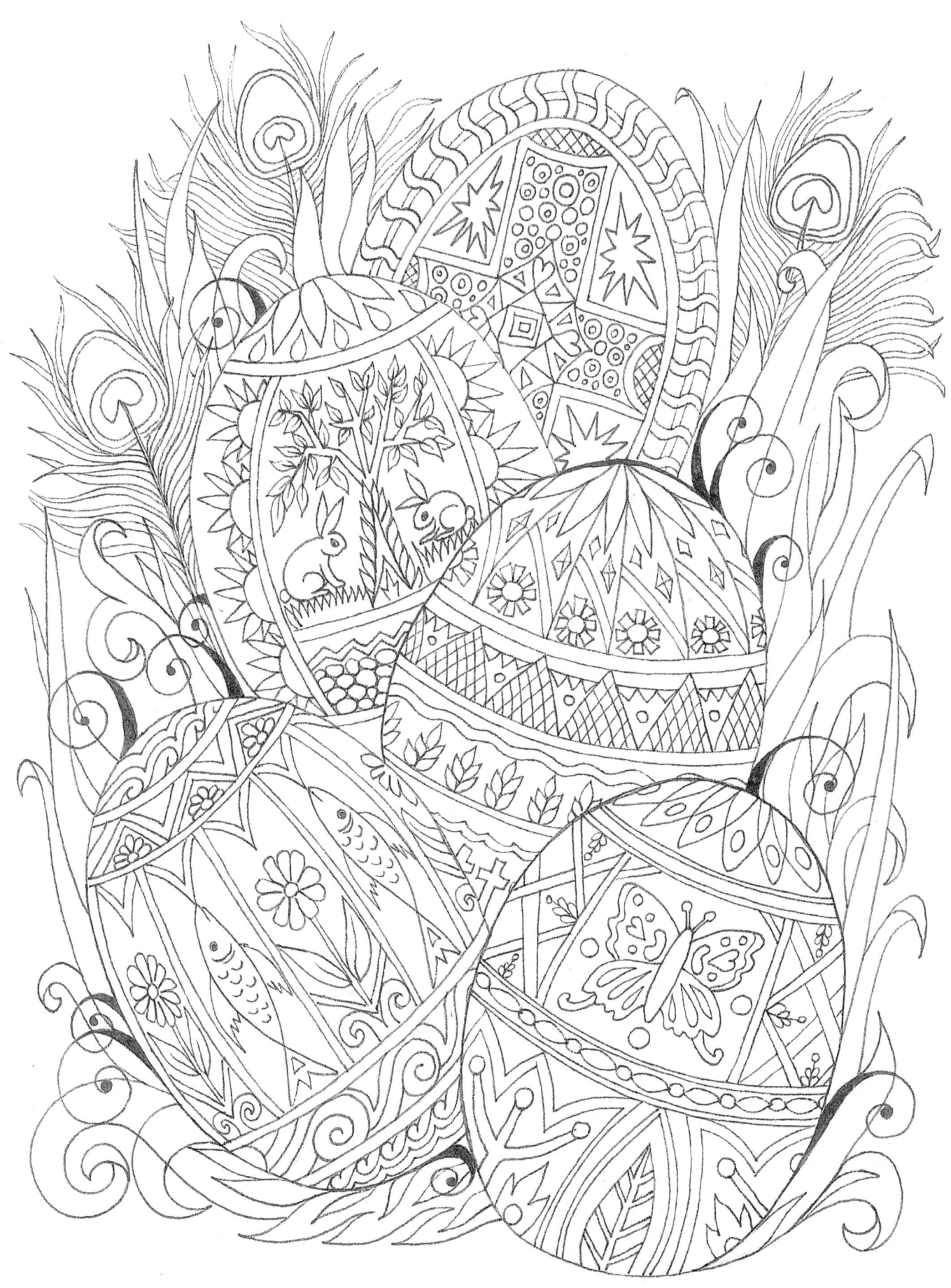

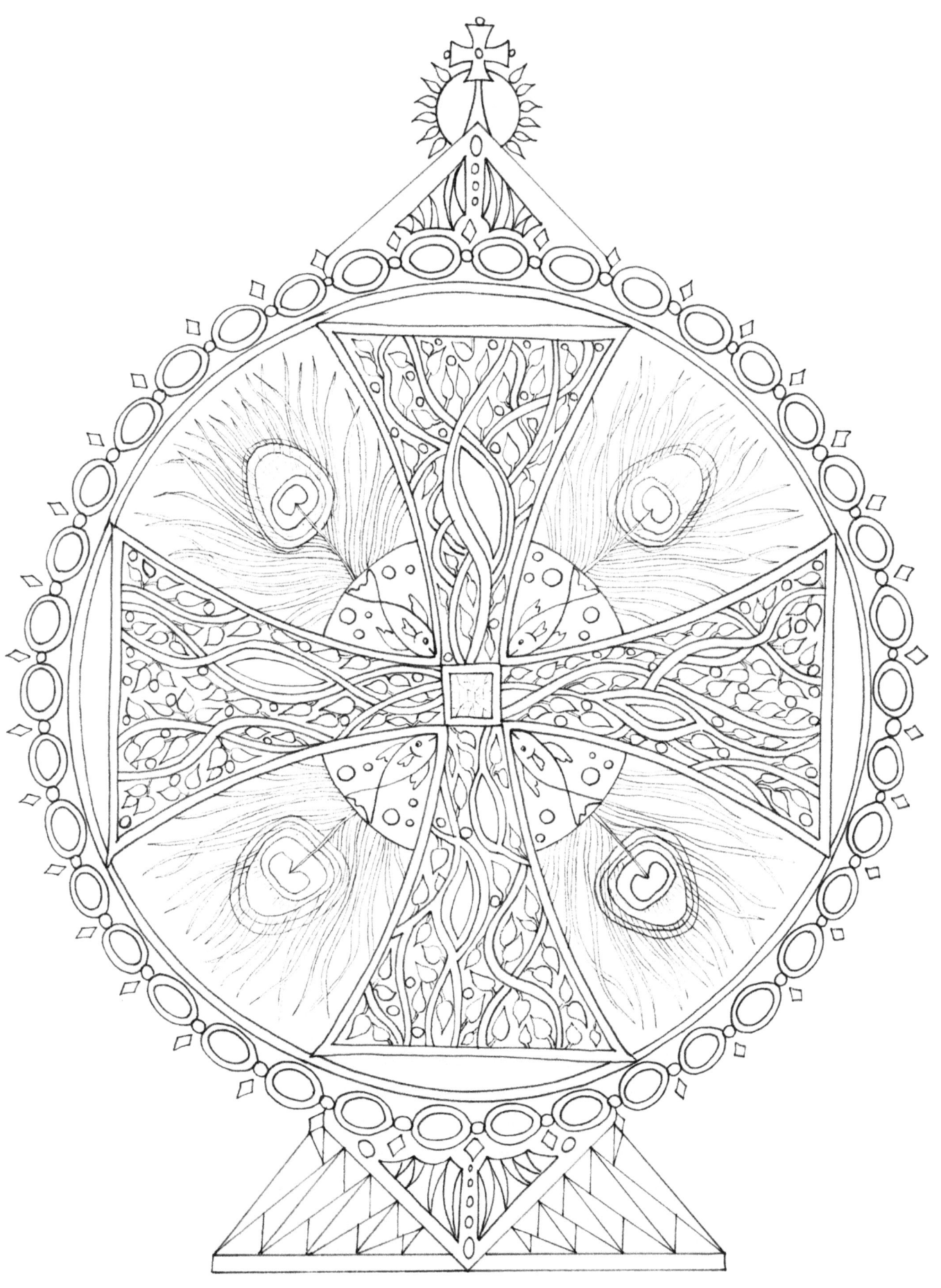

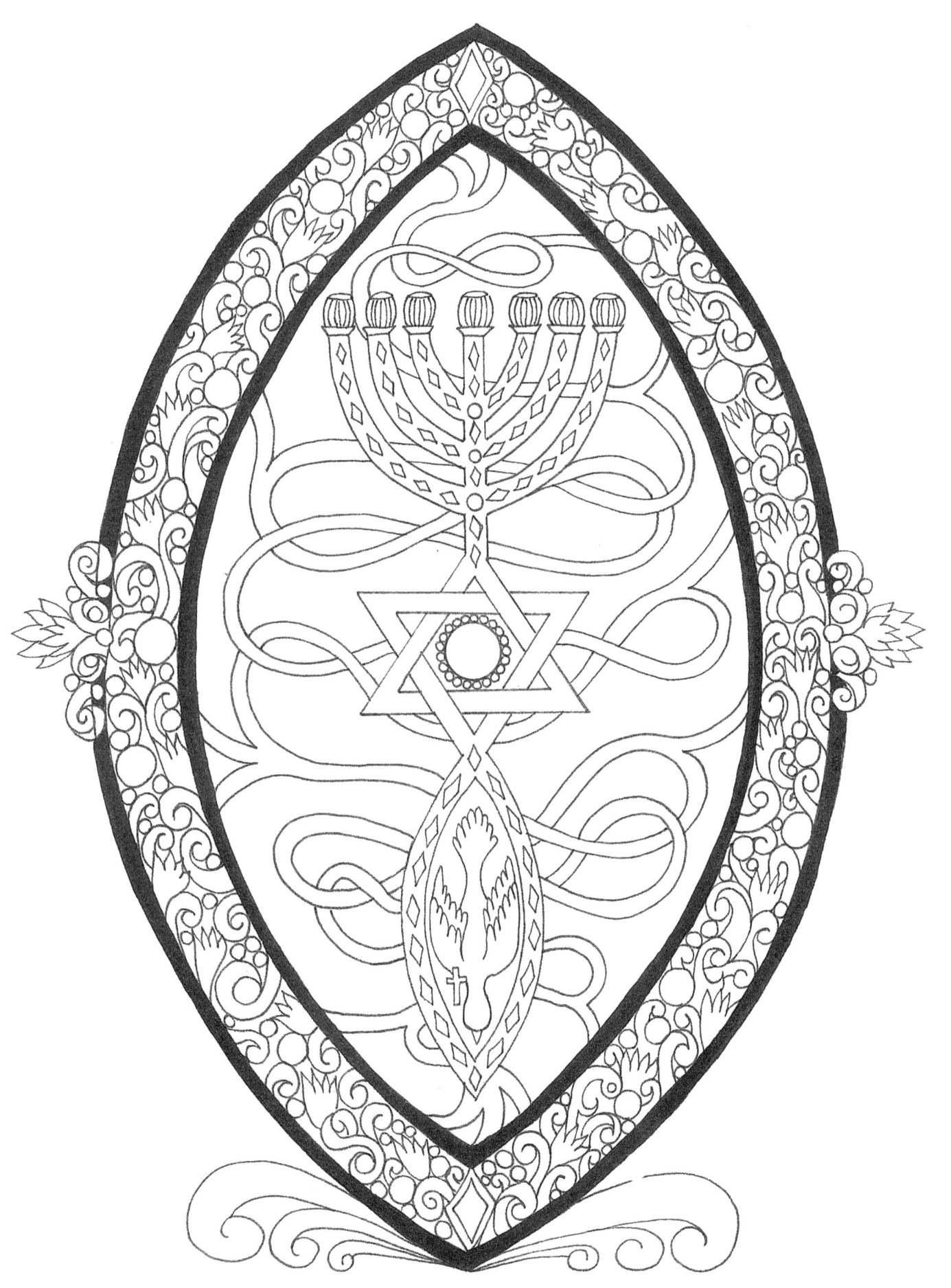

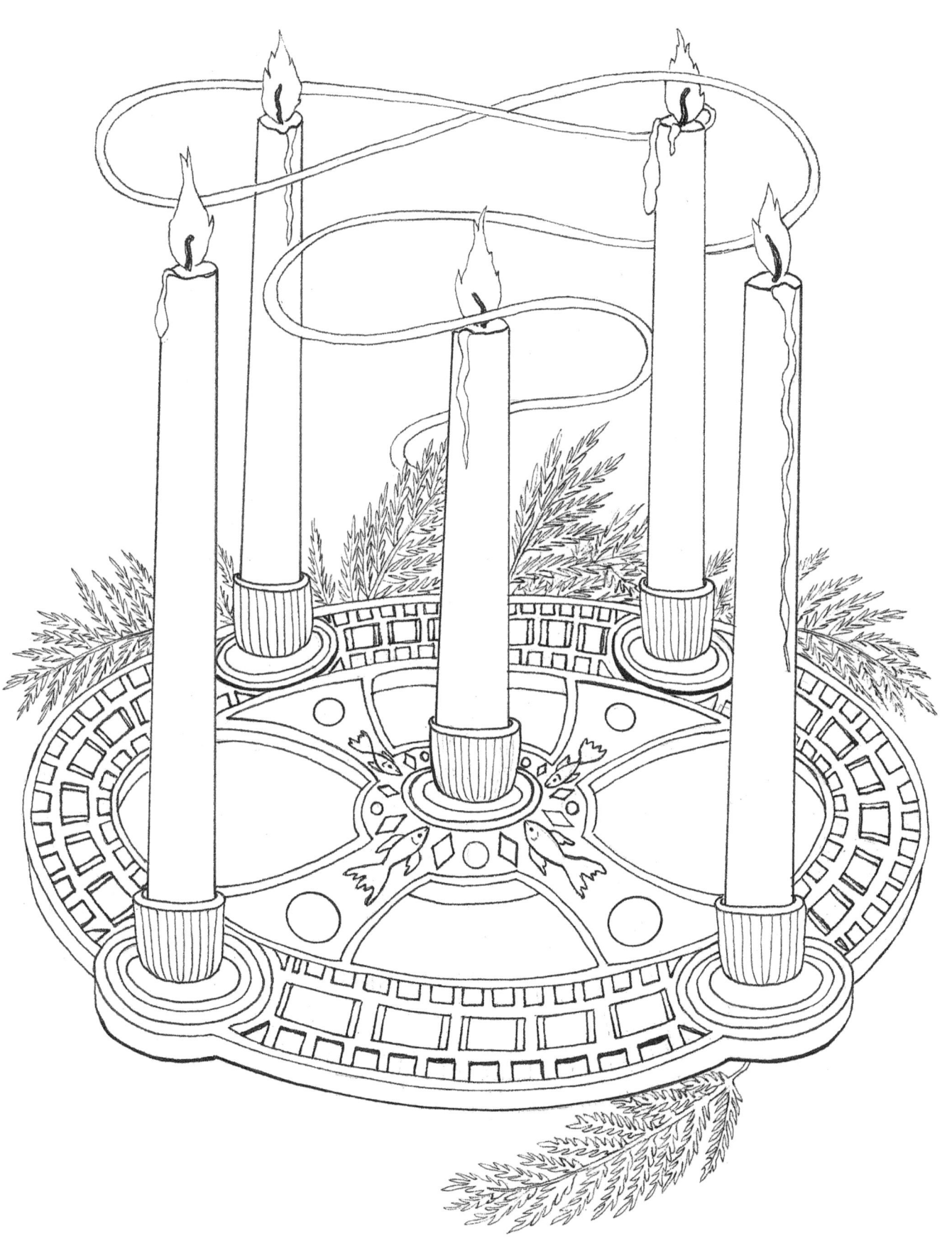

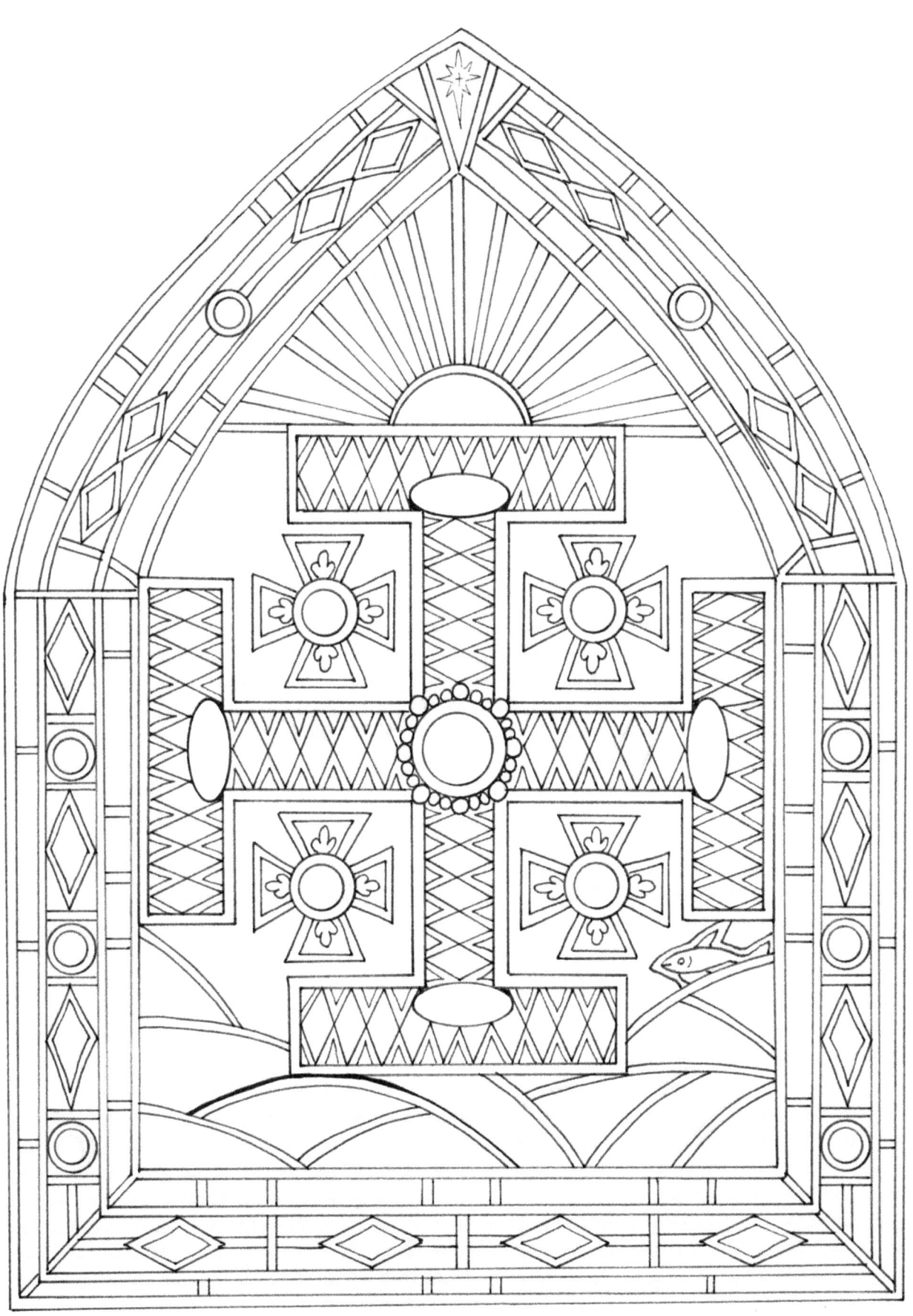

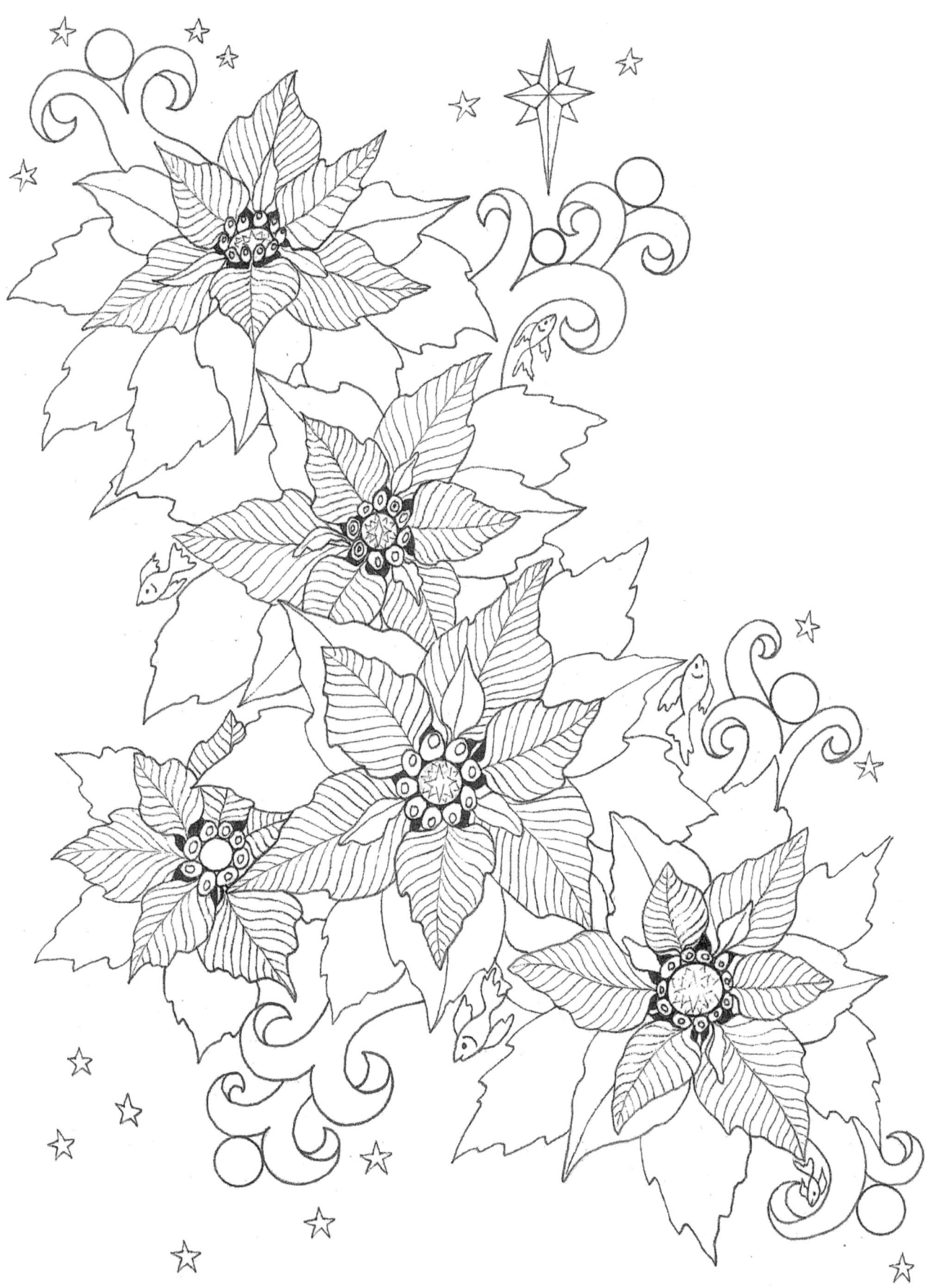

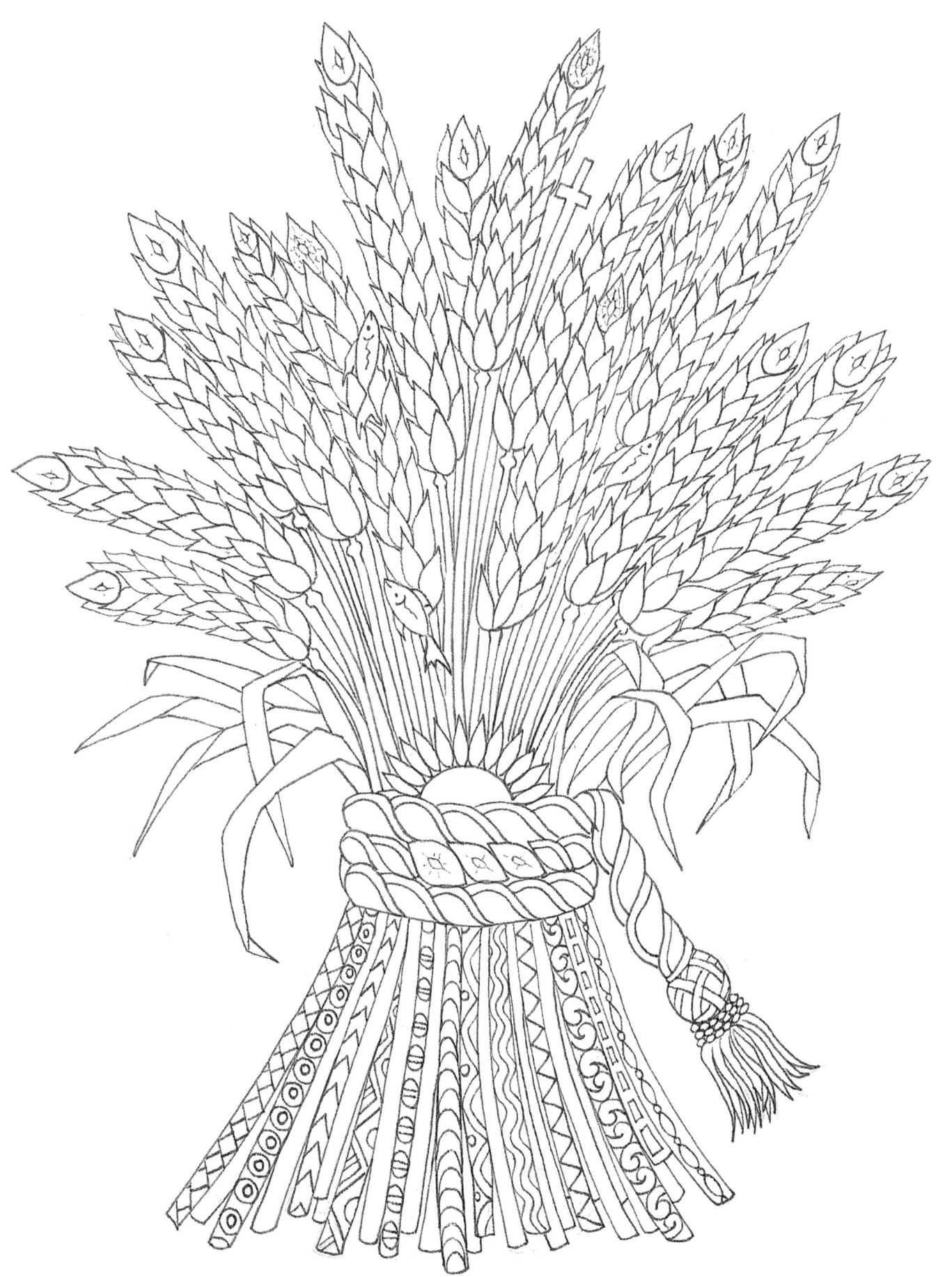

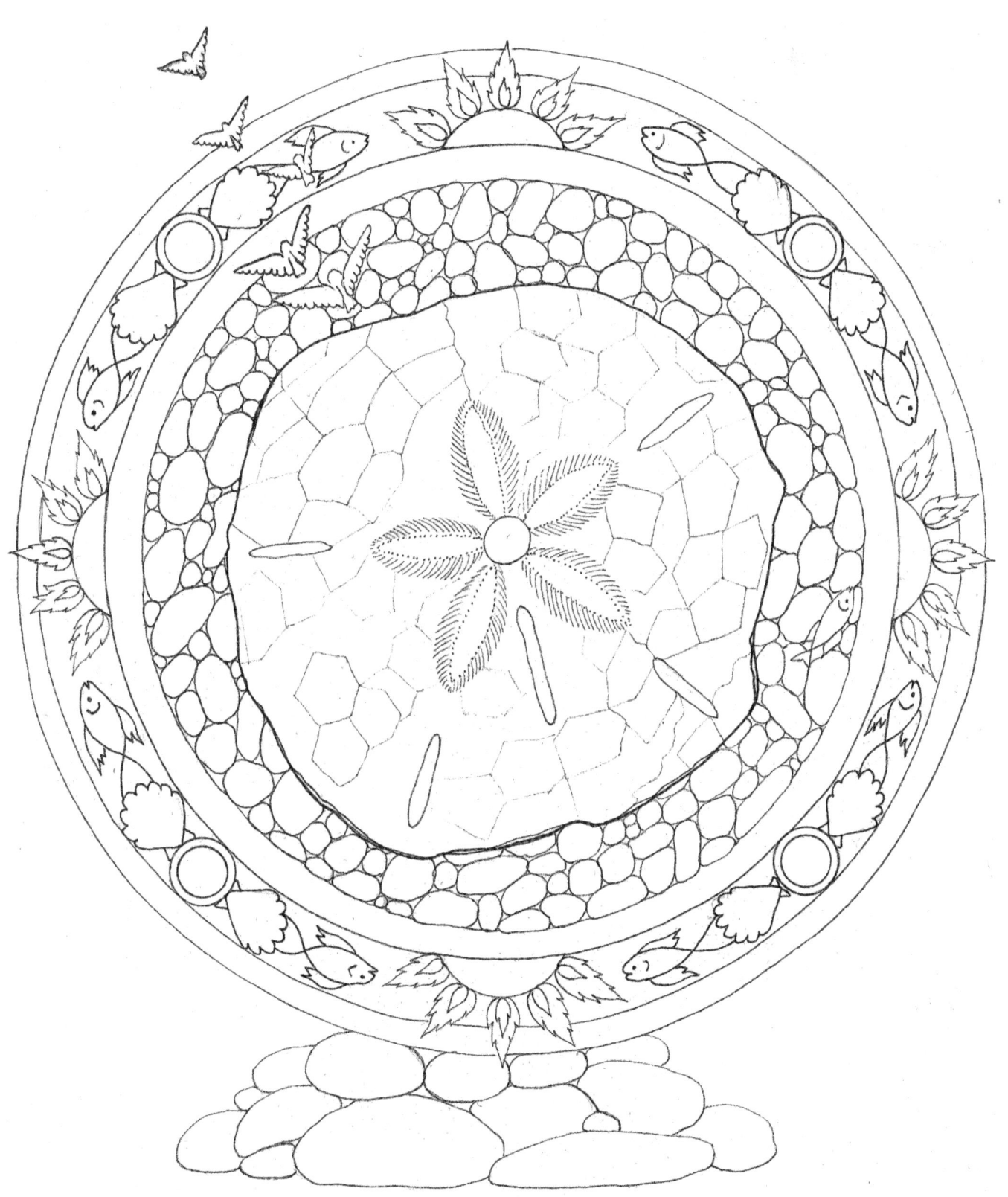

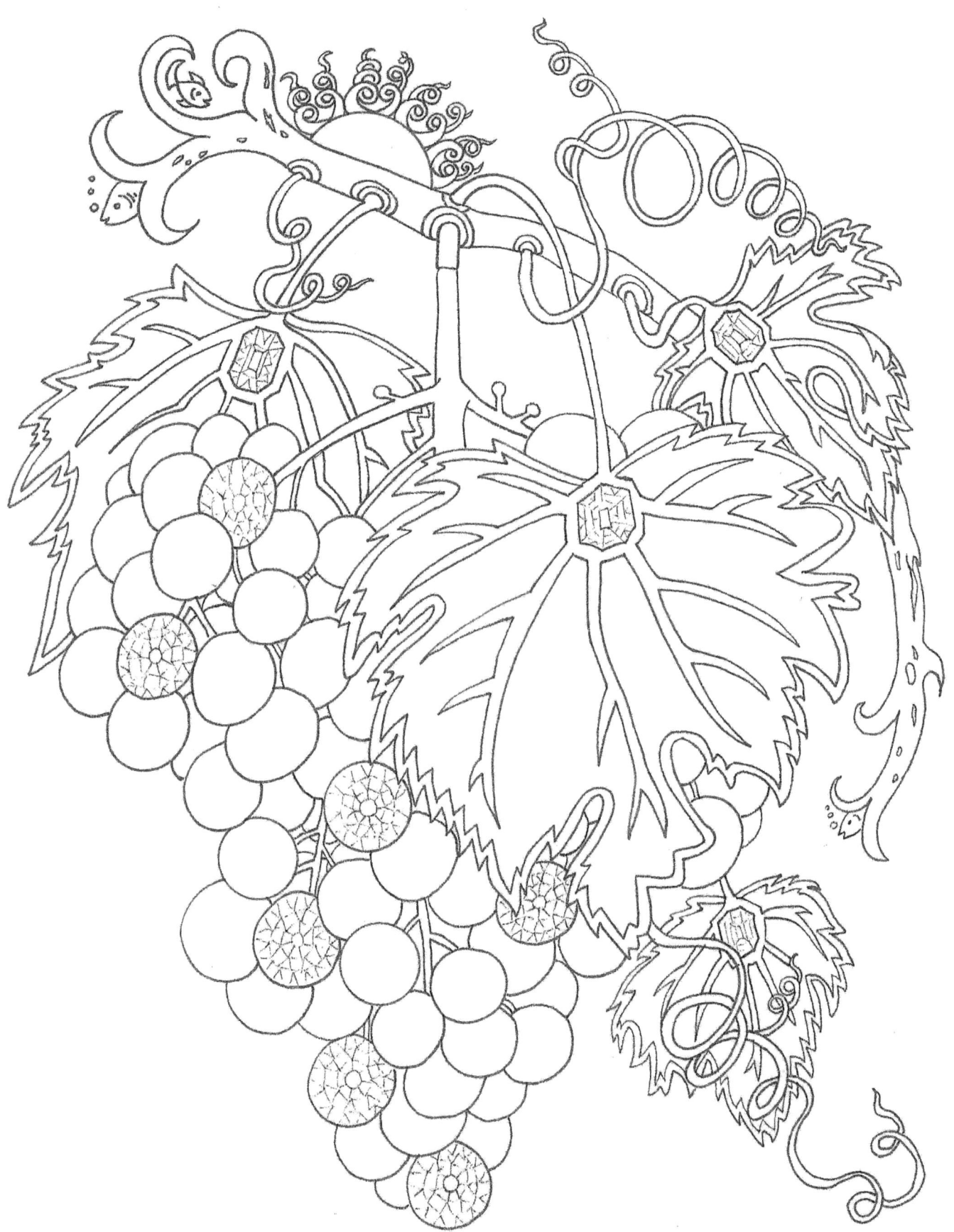

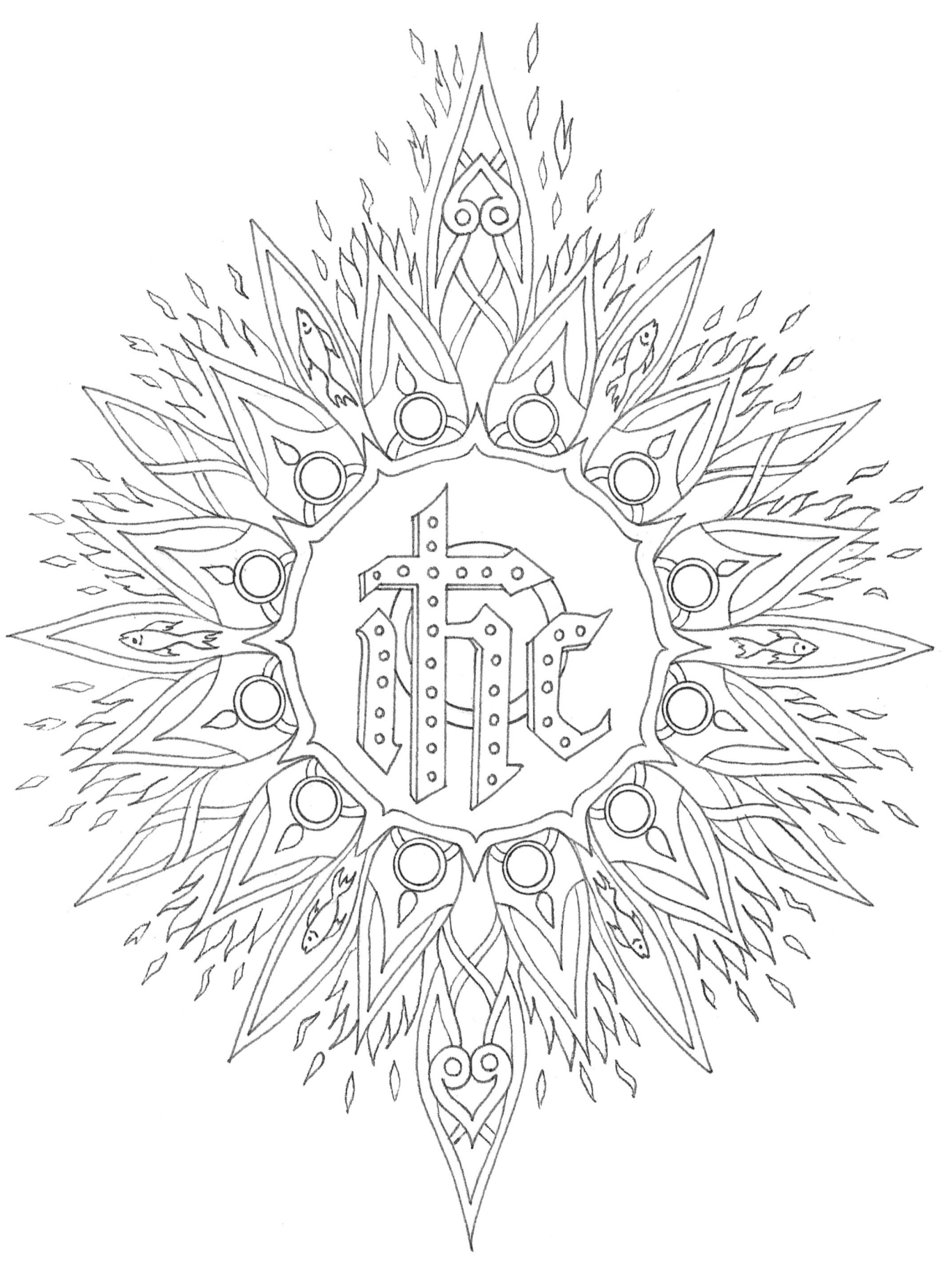

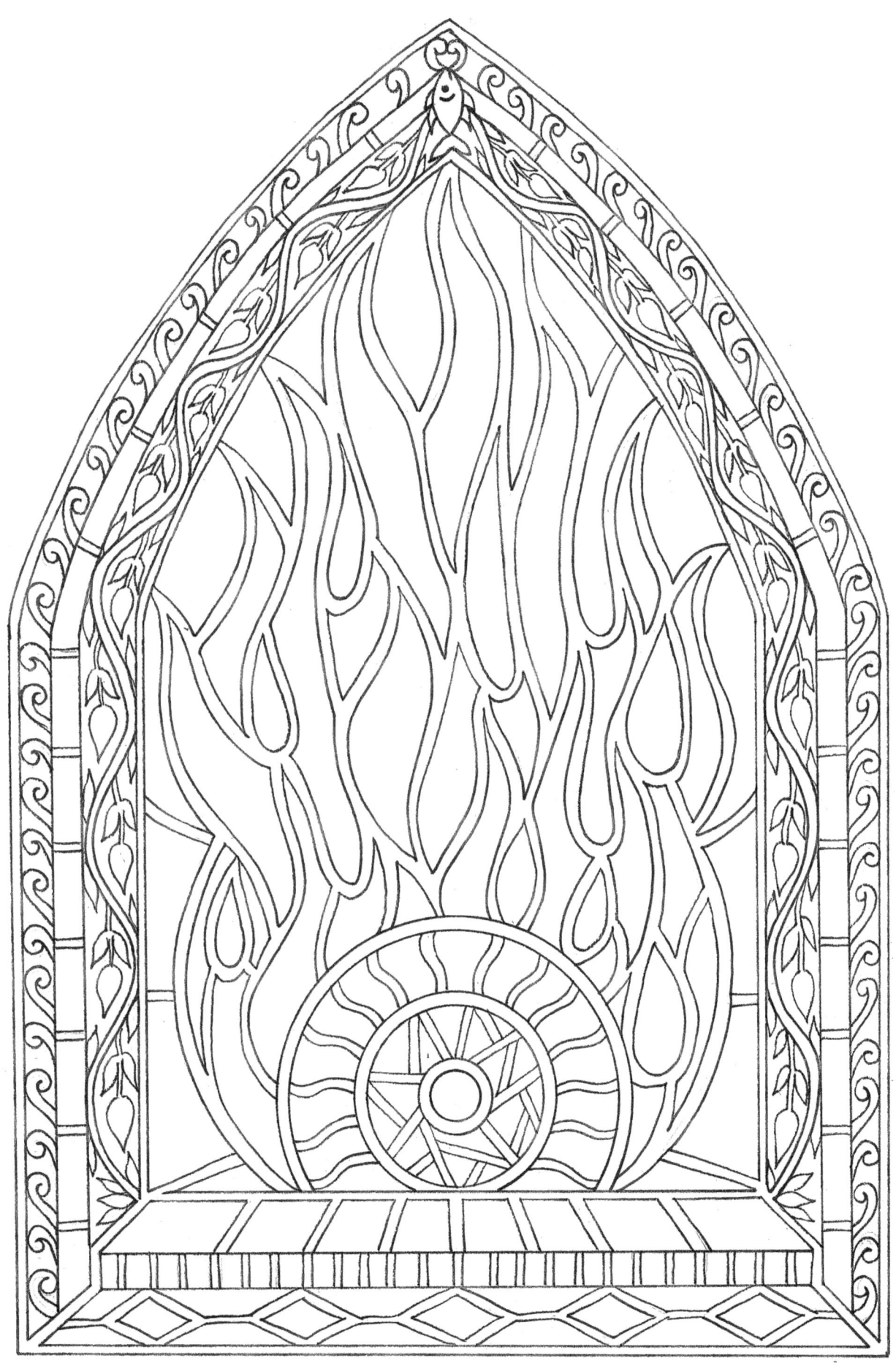

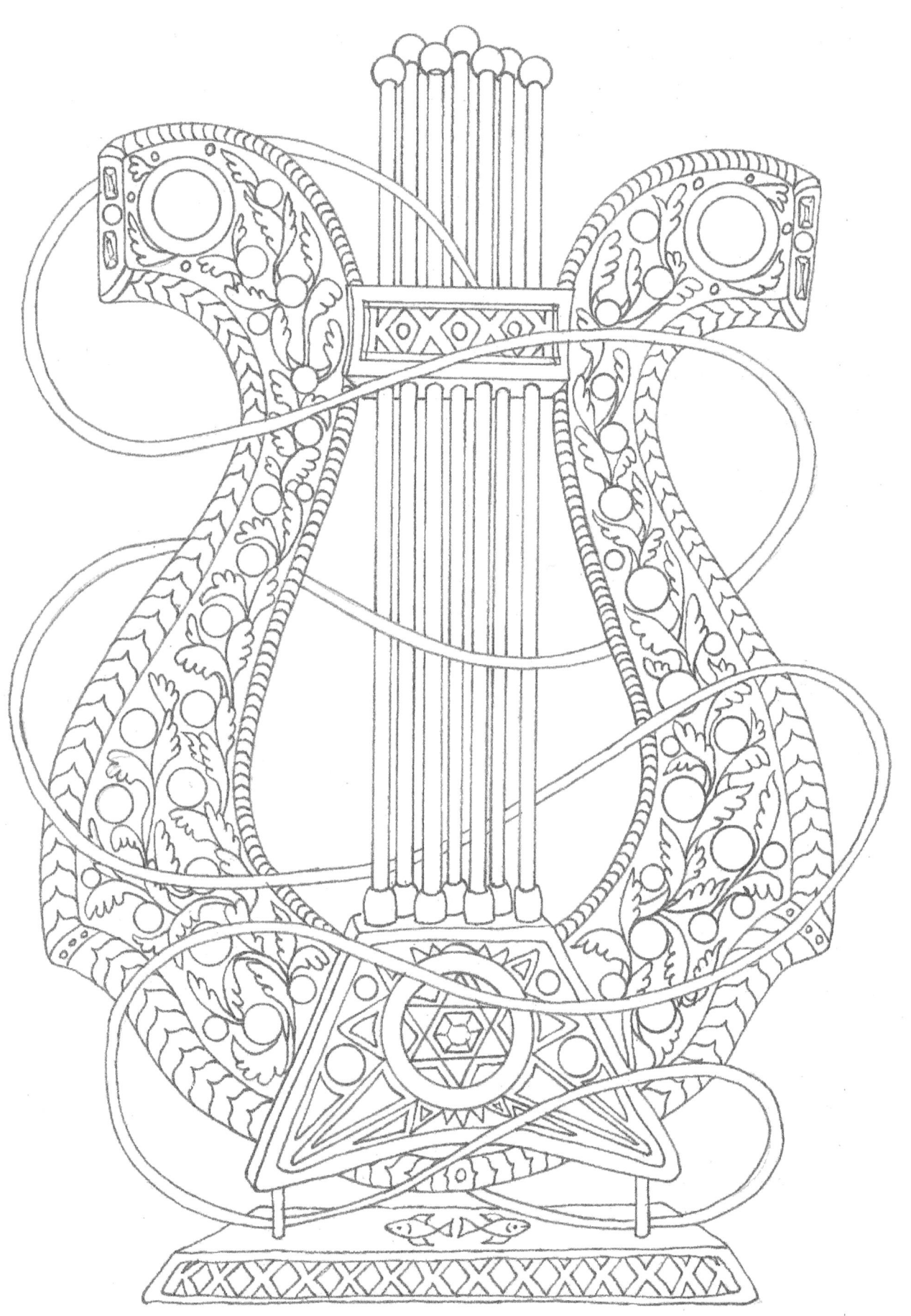

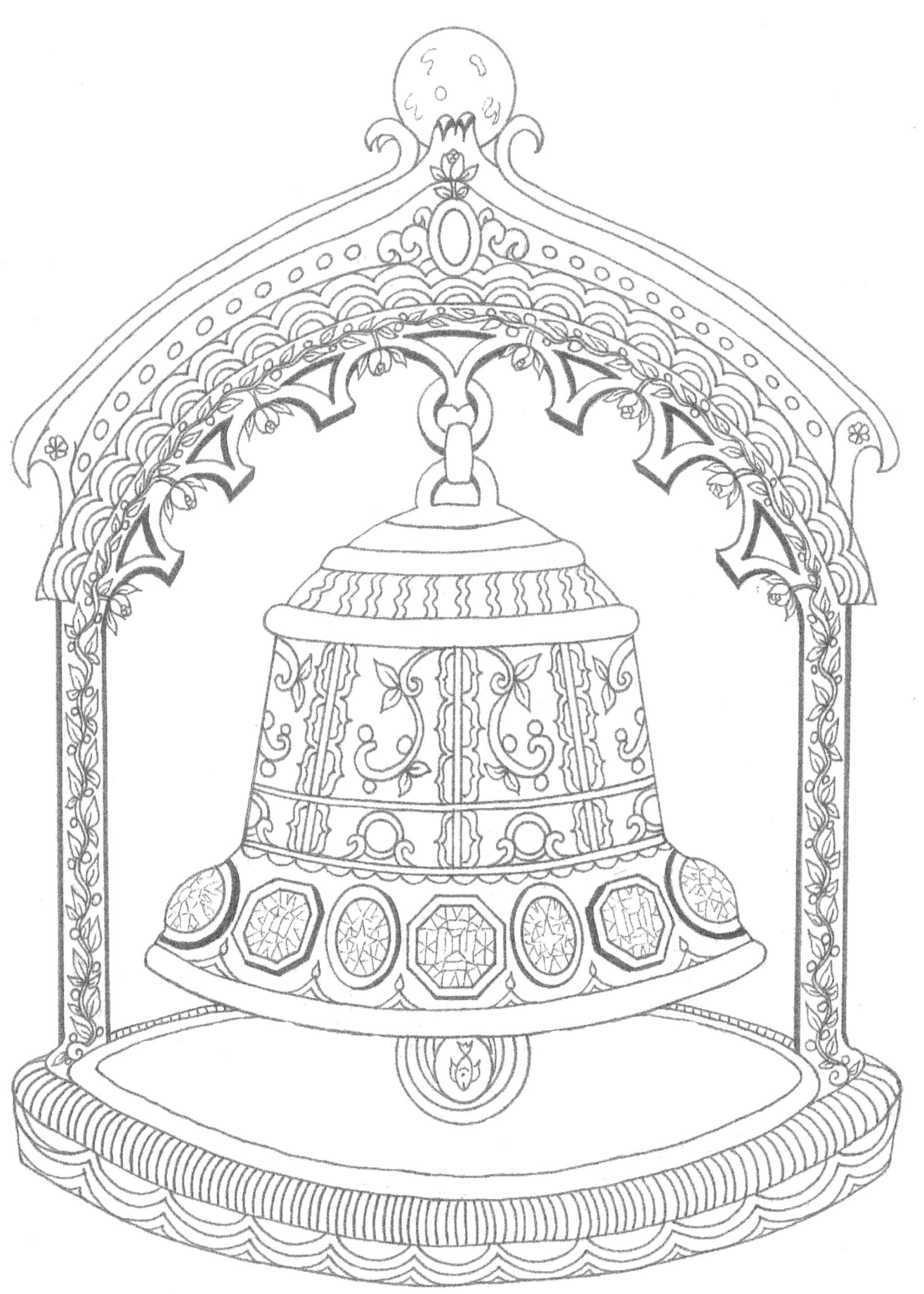

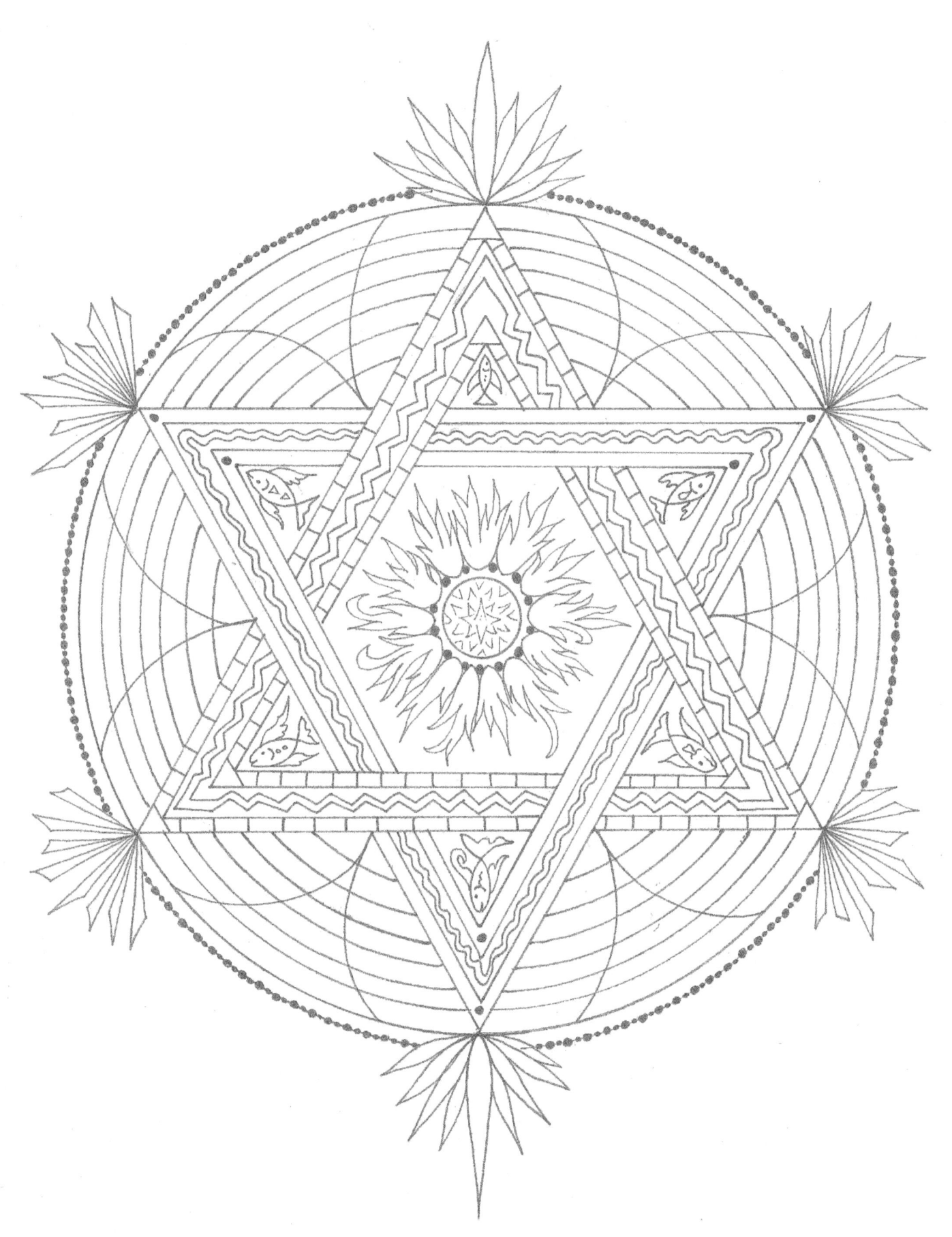

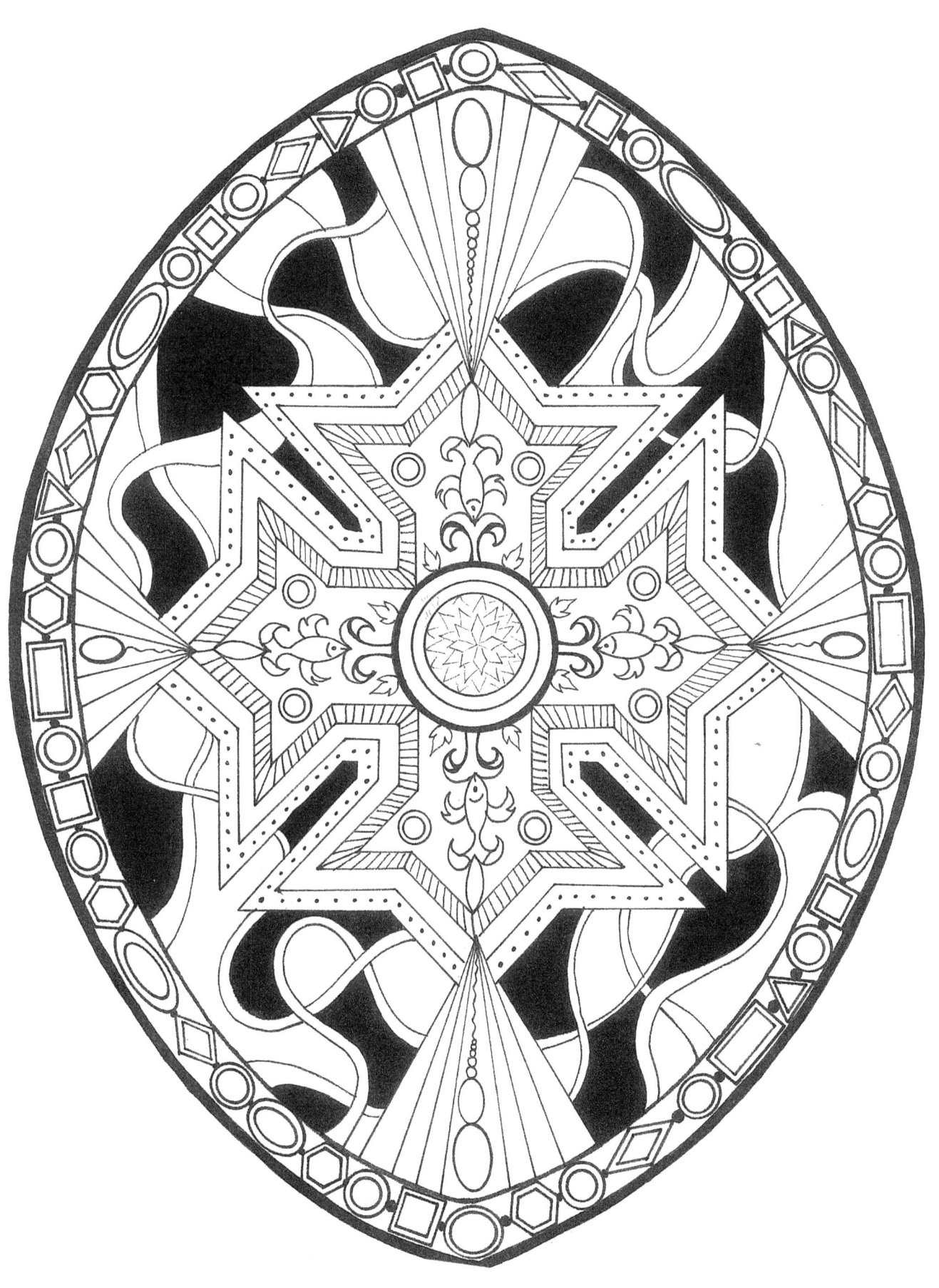

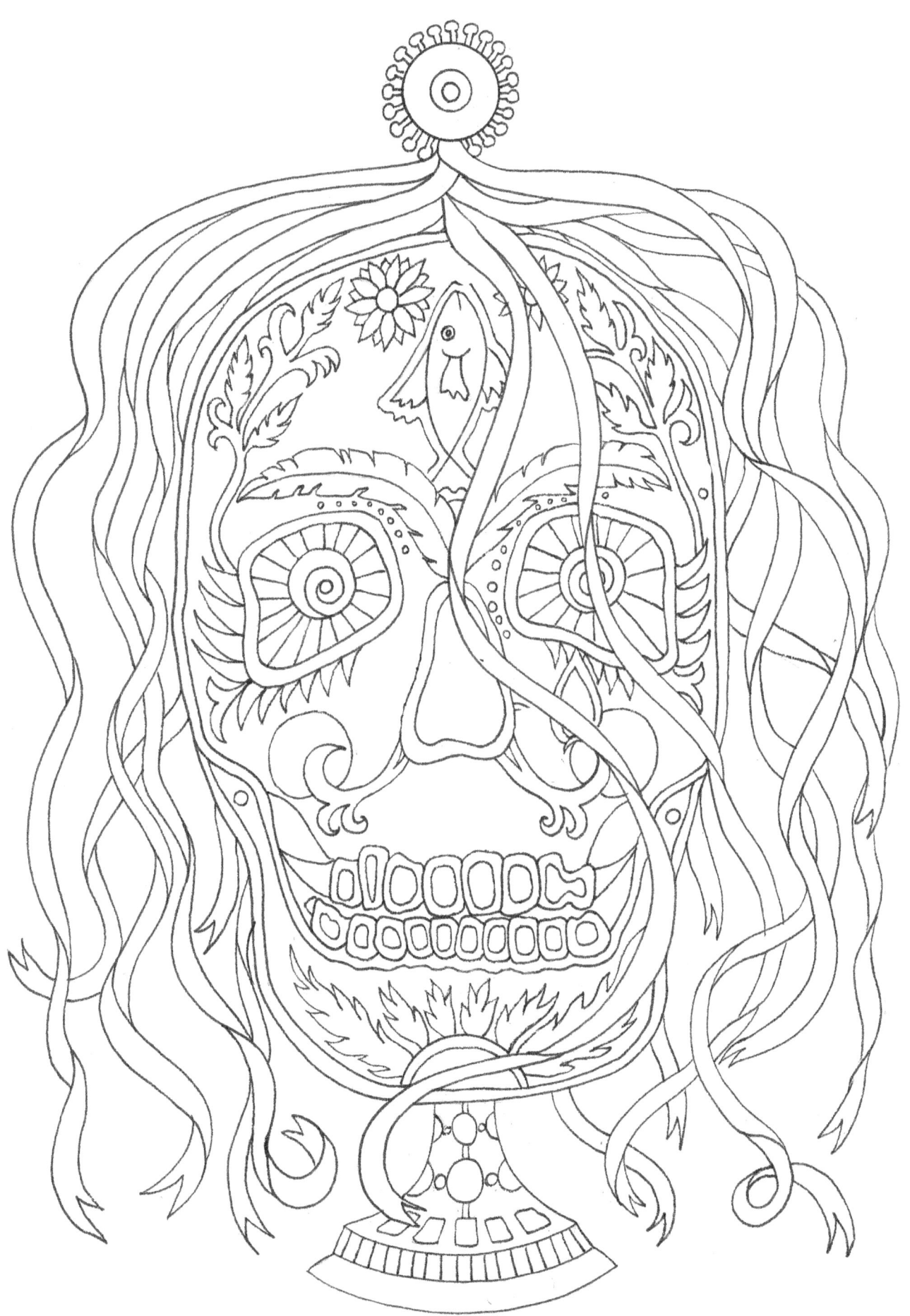

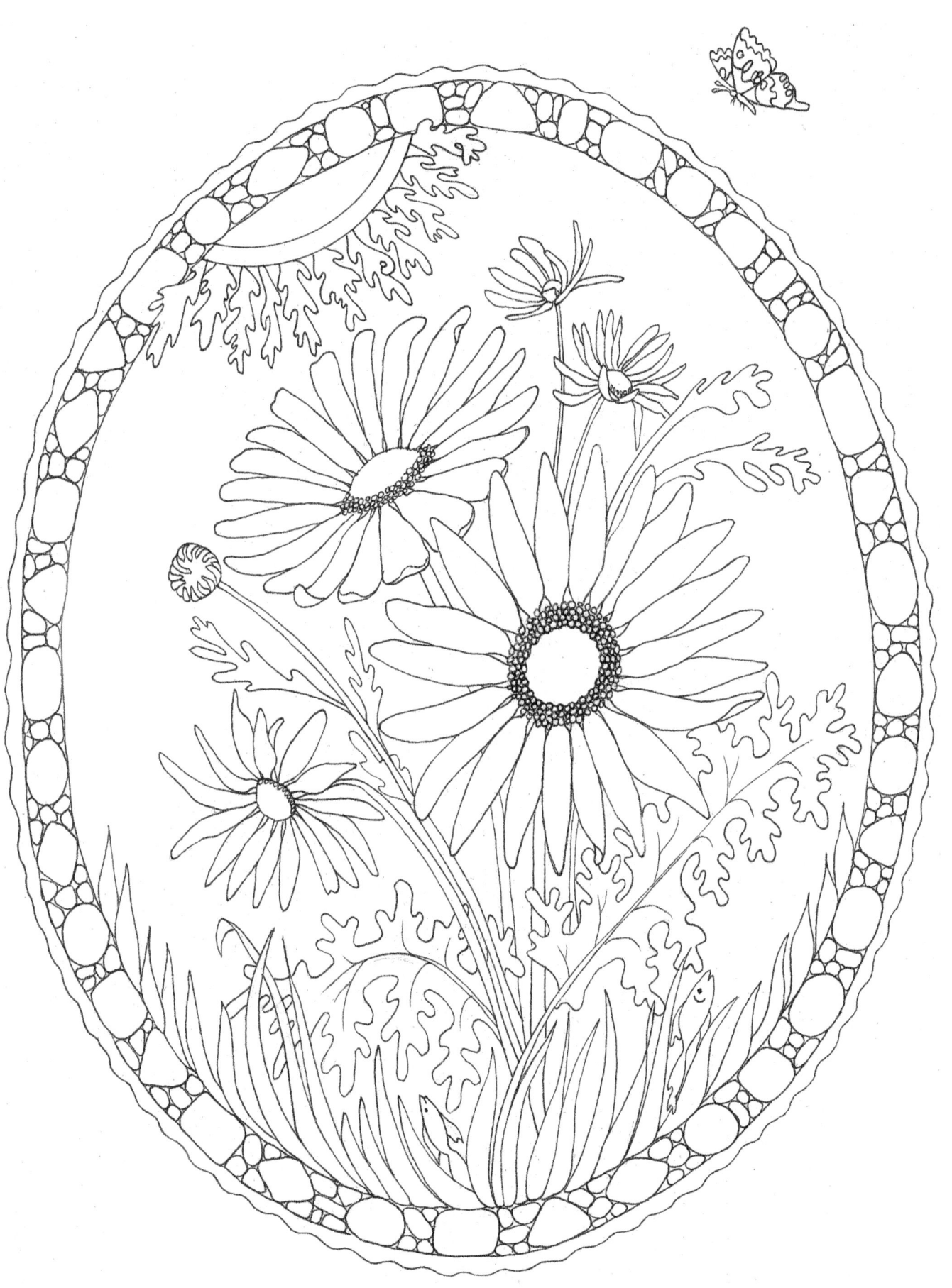

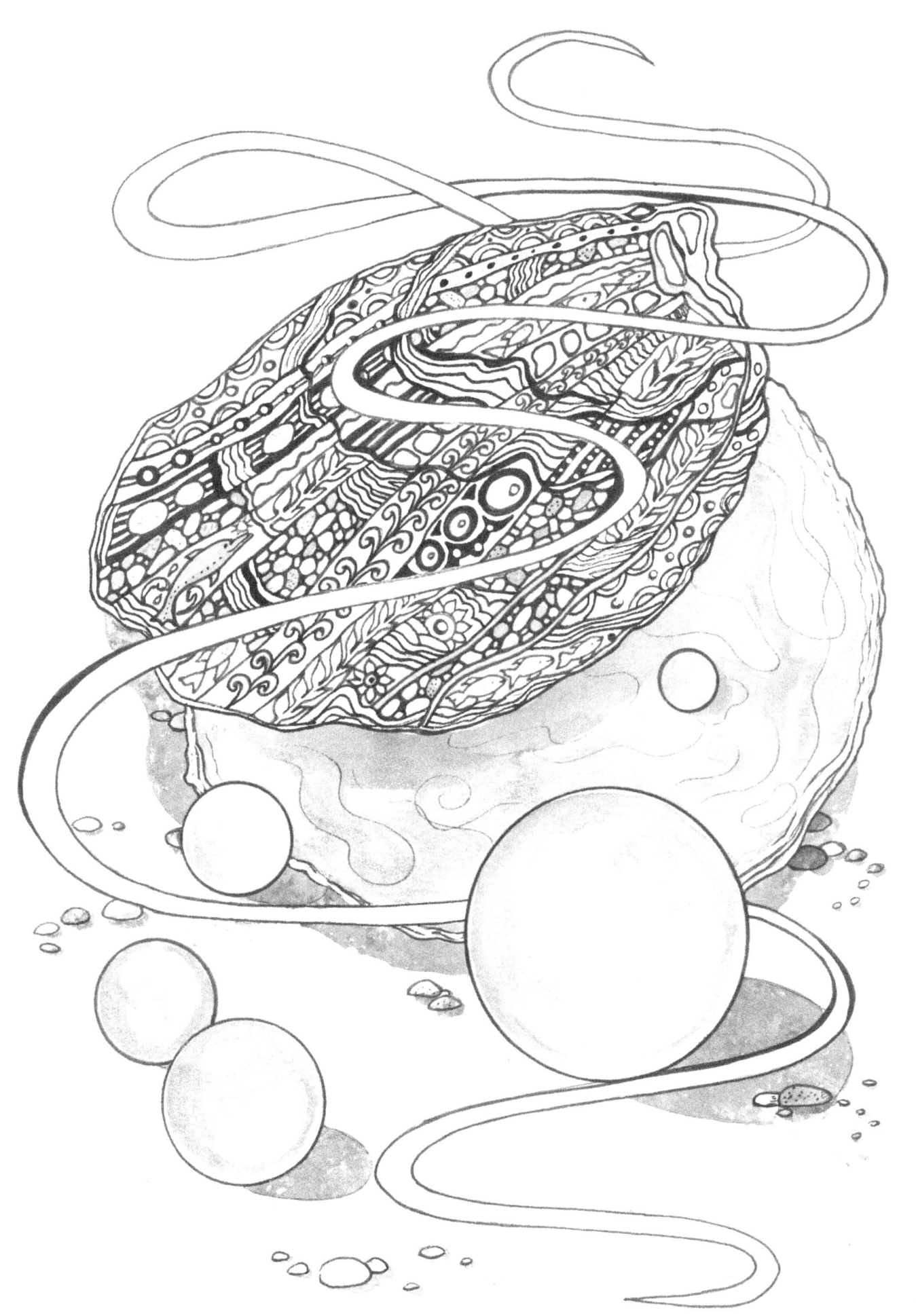

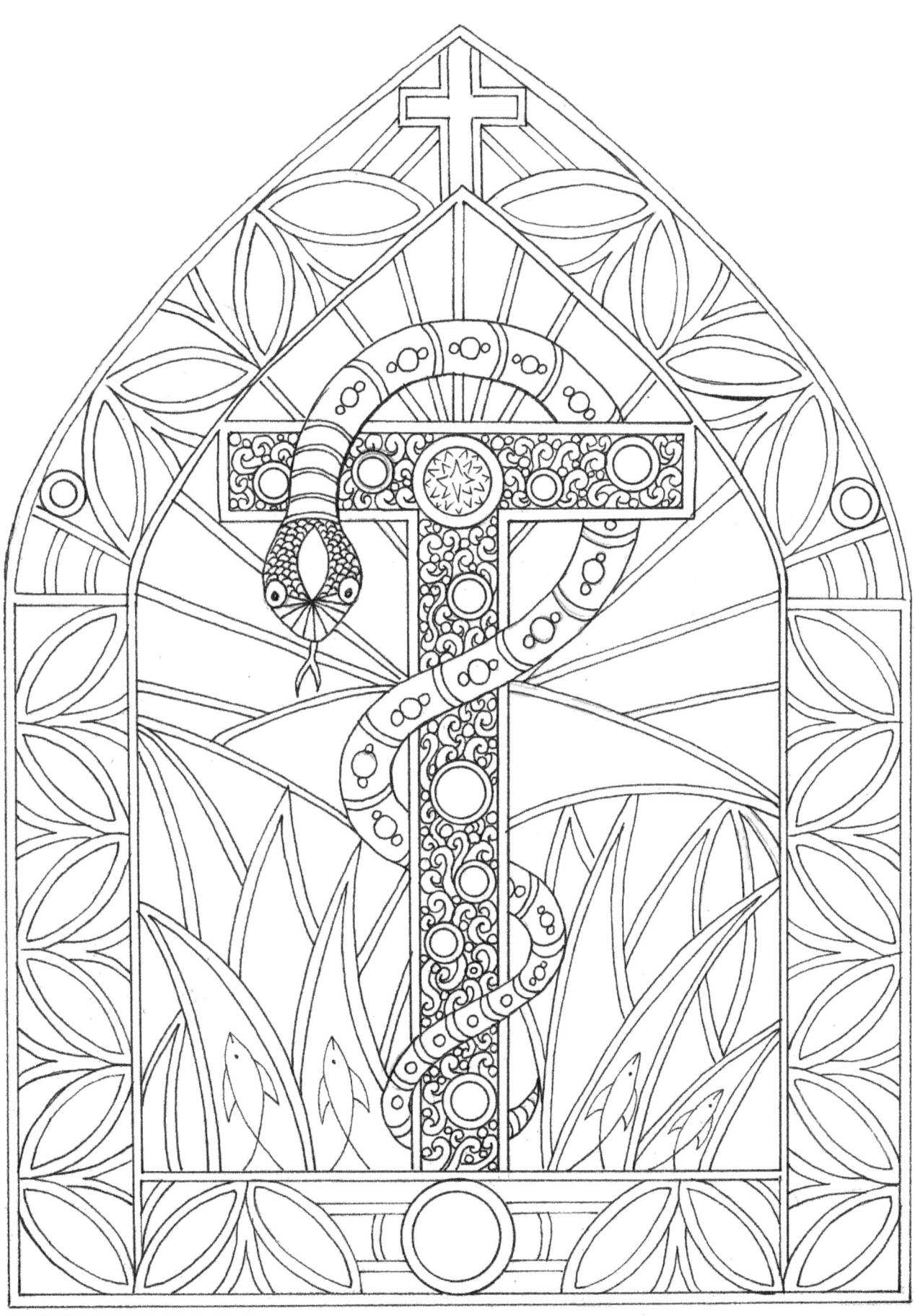

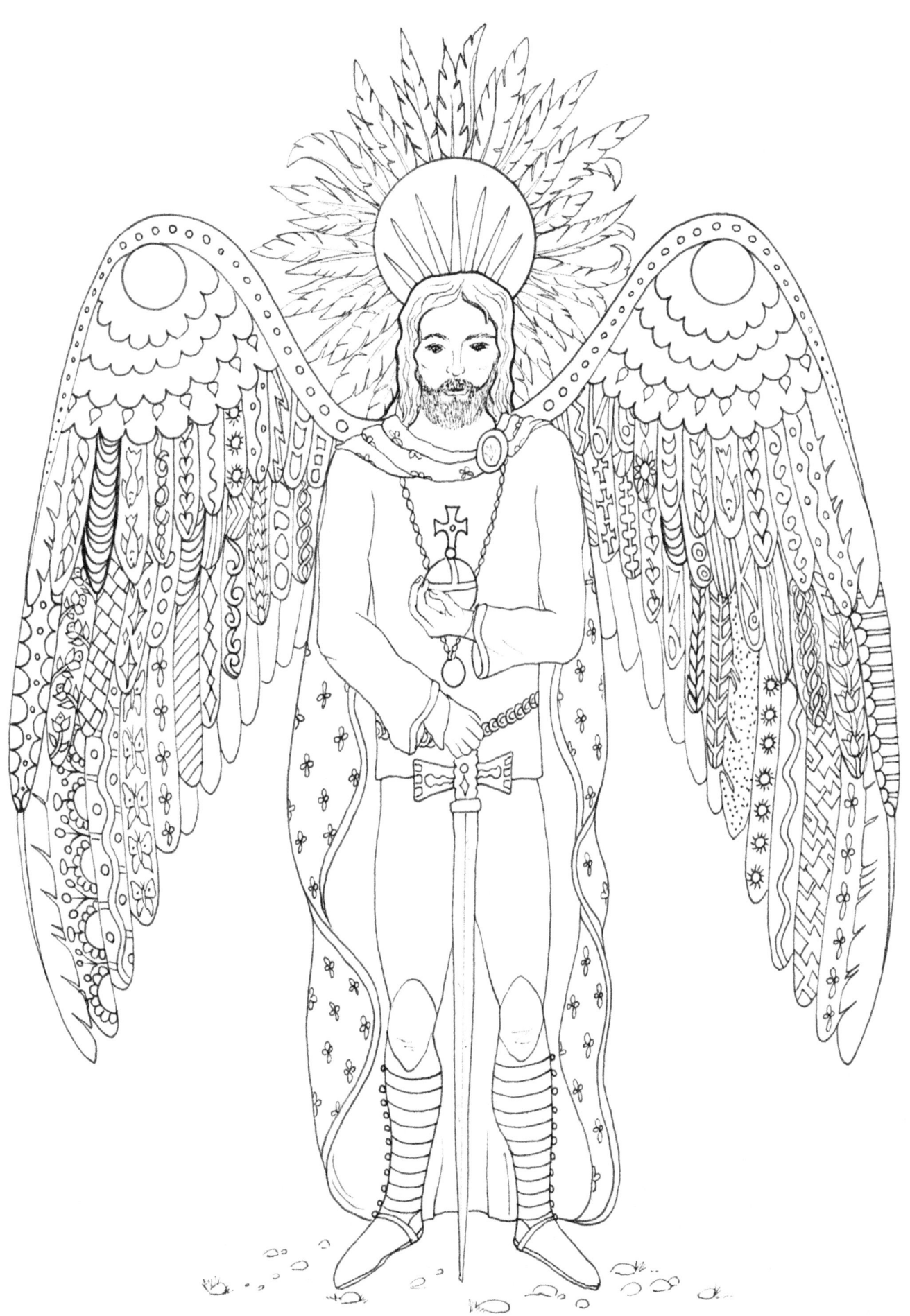

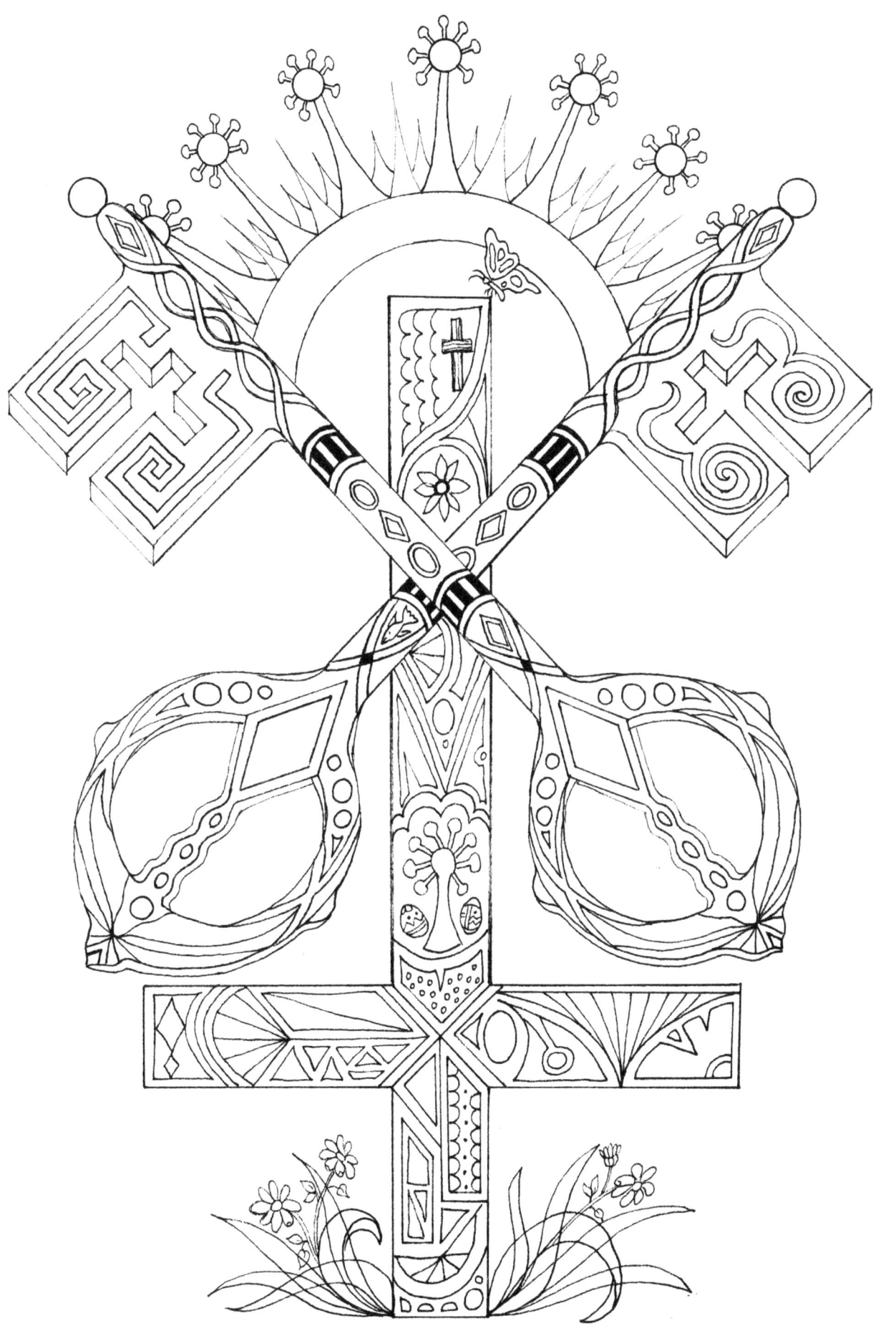

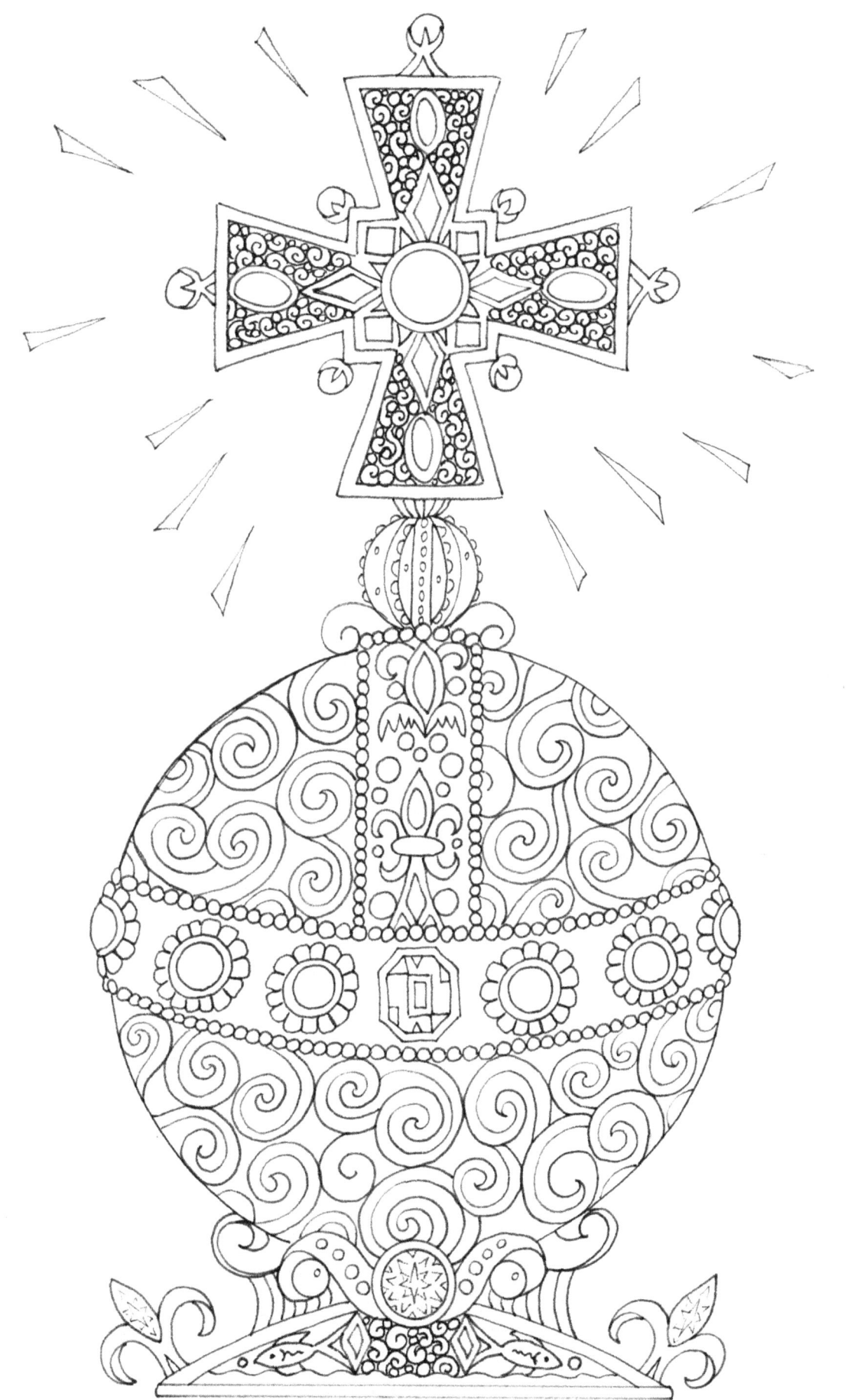

Page Number and
Summary of Meaning

Page

5   Dove: The one and only form the Holy Spirit is ever given in graphic representation, the dove in Christian iconography and art is used in representations of the baptism of Jesus, the Annunciation, and of Pentecost.

7   Latin Cross: The Latin cross is the most common of all forms of the cross. It is believed to be the style of cross on which Jesus died, and therefore is the almost universally accepted form of the cross in the Protestant church. The usual expression of it is plain, simple and unadorned, and is most often of wood construction.

9   Lamb of God (Agnus Dei): Recalling the ancient Hebrew temple sacrifices, the lamb symbolizes the meekness and innocence of Jesus as the perfect sacrificial offering to atone for the sins of the human family. In New Testament writings, it was John the Baptist who first used this metaphorical reference to Jesus when he said, "Look, the Lamb of God, who takes away the sin of the world" (John 1:29, NIV). Standing with a banner or lying on a book with seven seals, the lamb is one of the most important symbols ot the Christian faith.

11   Fish (Ichthus): This popular Christian symbol was used by early believers in the days of persecution as a secret sign of their shared faith. the initial letters of the phrase "Jesus Christ, Son of God, Savior" form the Greek word Ichthus, which means "fish." scratched on the walls of buildings or drawn on the floor in the sand, the symbol was frequently found engraved on the tombs of Christians buried in the catacombs of Rome.

13   Candelabrum (Menorah): Taken by adoption into the Christian treasury of faith, the candlestick is primarily understood to represent the eternal light of Christ, calling to mind the words of Jesus when he said: "I am the light of the world" and, secondarily, it signifies the Holy Spirit's seven gifts to baptized believers.

15   Crucifix: A cross bearing a representation of Jesus' body is one of the greatest icons of the Christian faith. By focusing on the sacrifice of Christ, The crucifix bears witness to the urgency of the gospel by clearly stating and affirming the depths of the mystery and meaning of the crucifixion.

17   Chi Rho: The Chi Rho is an ancient "sacred monogram" composed of the first two letters of "Khristos," the Greek word for "Christ" (XPICTOC). The letters "X" and "P" were eventually superimposed to form the symbol, pronounced "Key Ro." The Chi Rho monogram, in which early Christians identified the cross of Christ, figures prominently in the history of Christian symbology and manuscript illustration.

19   Rose: Frequently represented in gothic architecture in the form of a rose window, the rose has been a common Christian symbol since the 1200s. It is used to represent the Messianic promise, the nativity of Christ, the virgin Mary (her rose is white for purity), or martyrdom (a red rose).

21   Peacock: Since the flesh of a peacock was believed to be incorruptible and thus beyond decay, this fascinating bird with a "thousand eyes" became a strong symbol of immortality and eternal life. And accordingly, because the male peacock sheds its feathers every year and grows new, brighter plumage, the favoured bird came to represent Christ in his Resurrection. The iridescent "eyes" on the bird's fan tail were seen to symbolize the all-seeing eye of God.The symbolism of the peacock was adopted early in Christian history and has been found on the tombs and walls of the catacombs in Rome. In time, it became popular in 0sacred architecture and has enjoyed wide distribution in Christian paintings, stained glass windows, tapestry and illuminated manuscripts, as well as on everyday objects like lamps and dinnerware.

23   Celtic cross: It is believed that in his preaching, St. Patrick in the fifth century encountered a sacred stone marked with the circle of the sun goddess, and made the sign of the Latin cross through it. With that gesture, the saint is credited with having created a symbol that linked the life-giving properties of the sun with the saving power of the Christian cross. It was a gesture that is often viewed as a merging of a pagan symbol with the growing popularity of the Christian cross in its simplest form. The Celtic cross features a ring surrounding the intersection of the arms of the Latin cross, the Roman cross of execution in its most basic form.

25   Tri-Fish: In the graphic conceptualization of the Tri-Fish,, this celebrated and universally embraced image of the fish as a symbol of Christ is raised to another level when it is thus presented in a unified form with two other fish that all together symbolize the Trinity: God the Father and the God the Holy Spirit.

27   Passion Flower: The richly endowed Passion flower has come to represent the scourging, crowning with thorns, and crucifixion of Jesus. This natural wonder was discovered in his travels by a humble Mexican friar who submitted it in a painting to a monastic scholar in Rome. The Roman scholar included it in a book about the Passion of Christ, and after that, the flower rapidly became a treasured symbol of Christian the Christian church.

29   Scroll: The scroll holds within itself the words, the Voice of God, which constitutes more than an awesome sound; the words indicate an occurrence, a happening, an event, the beginning of circumstance; the entrance of Eternity into the realm of the temporal.

31   Eagle: The eagle's association with the sun, fire, and light, together with its strength, endurance and power to soar over, above and beyond, became a strong image of Christian immortality, as well as a figure of the Messiah. The eagle's association with regeneration and renewal, strength and endurance, gave rise, therefore, to its standing as an unambiguous symbol of Christ the Redeemer and of regeneration of the believer through the waters of baptism.

33   Loaves and Fishes: Among the symbols used by the early Christians in decorating the tombs of their cemeteries, those relating to the practice of Holy Communion were prominent. Of these, the earliest and favourite symbol was that inspired by the miracle of the multiplication of the loaves and fishes. The strong image of the loaves and the fishes brings to mind the observance of Holy Communion, and therefore of the transformation into the spiritual energy it embodies when consumed within the context of belief.

35   Fleur-de-lis: French for "lily flower," the fleur-de-lis is a plant that bears blossoms composed of three petals and three sepals mounted on an erect stalk. Like the shamrock, the fleur-de-lis is a natural phenomenon that proclaims the deep mystery of the Godhead, the essential purity of which was planted in the soul of the Blessed Virgin.

37   Lantern: Just as oil lamps, flames, candles and lampstands are symbols of the presence of God before and with his people, so too are lanterns. While not as widely used or recognized as a Christian symbol, the lantern nevertheless holds steady with the same sacred significance as the other symbols mentioned: that is, the lantern proclaim Jesus as the light of the world illuminating and bringing focus to the story of salvation.

39   Scallop Shell: The scallop shell is a beloved Christian symbol referring to the baptism of believers generally and to that of Jesus specifically. The shell is commonly depicted on baptismal fonts, while the dish used to pour water over the heads of baptismal candidates is often an actual scallop shell, or at least in the shape of one. The three water droplets falling from the shell symbolize the Trinity; that Christian baptism is performed in the name of the Father, the Son and the Holy Spirit.

41   Dolphin: Because the dolphin was thought to be loving and tender toward humans, it came early in the history of the church to be embraced as a symbol of Christian belief. Often seen swimming alongside ships, the dolphin was familiar to sailors and regarded as a guide, rescuer and friend. It suggested to sailors the image of Jesus protecting believers from the dangers of the storm-tossed waters of life, of rescuing the shipwrecked, of saving them from the depths of depravity and sin, and finally of bringing them to the safety of heaven's shore.

43   Ox: Regarded as a symbol of strength, patience, and endurance the ox was ready for its destiny as a beast of burden in bearing a yoke and pulling a plough, or of offering itself as a sacrifice on an altar of atonement. For this reason, the ox became a fitting symbol of the life and work of Christ, who on one occasion invited his followers to take upon themselves his yoke, which he promised would easy to bear. Fitting also, because his Messianic presence on earth culminated in his sacrificial and atoning death on the cross.

45   Anchor Cross: Because the "stock" at the top of a typical anchor is cast in the shape of a cross, the anchor was used during the early days of Christian persecution as a signature of belief in disguise.

47   Budded Cross: Each arm of the Budded cross is intended to depict the Holy Trinity, while all twelve together can be read to make reference to the "budding" apostles of Jesus.

49   Bee, Hive and Honeycomb: A relatively modern symbol, the bee is sometimes viewed as an emblem of Christ, with the sweetness of its honey representing his grace, mercy and forgiveness. More often, however, the bee is symbolic of tireless industry and diligence, and the beehive of a perfectly ordered and well-functioning community in which all its members are vigilant in carrying out their prescribed duties. This interpretation also suggests that the bee represents individual Christians, and the hive the church of Christ.

51   Pelican: Common in Christian art, the pelican is a symbol of the Atonement, and of Christ the Redeemer. It is based on the legend that in times of famine, the mother pelican opens her breast and feeds her young with her own blood. The bird is therefore a graphic symbol of the mystery of Christ and of the Holy Communion in which Christians are revived and nourished by the body and blood of Christ the Redeemer.

53   Butterfly: In a life cycle that moves the insect from an earth-crawling caterpillar to a seemingly lifeless chrysalis encased within a cocoon, and finally to the complete transformation of winged resplendence, the butterfly reminded early Christians of the promise of their own physical metamorphosis upon the return of Christ. The butterfly, therefore, symbolizes the life, death and resurrection of Jesus, as well as the ultimate rising of all believers to a new life in a new creation.

55   Conqueror's Cross: The significance of this monogram in Christian belief is that "Jesus Christ the Conqueror" is victorious over sin and death; that he is the Everlasting Lord, and Ultimate Ruler of heaven and earth.

57   Lion: The symbolic reference of the lion to Christ was enhanced by the ancient myth that lion cubs are born dead but come to life three days later when the male lion breathes on the young cubs, a tale which reminded early Christians of the Resurrection.

59   Lily: This trumpet-shaped white flower, which bursts from a seemingly lifeless bulb in spring, is first of all and primarily a powerful symbol of the Christ's resurrection.

61   Borromean Rings: As a symbol of Christian belief, the circle represents perfection, infinity, and eternity, attributes expressed by the omnipotent and eternal God in his act of creating a multiplicity of phenomena in a circularform, including the sun, the moon, and the planets. Formed of three interlocking circles, the Borromean Rings form a symbol for the Trinity. The circles represent the eternal nature of the Father, Son and Holy Spirit. Entwined, they remind us that God is one, even though he reveals himself in three Persons.

63   Crown and Cross: A cross passing through a crown is a traditional Christian symbol of victory appearing in many churches. The crown of thorns, mockingly placed on the brow of the crucified Lord, is transformed into a bejeweled crown of royalty, heralding Christ upon his resurrection as King and announcing his final defeat of death. The crown is also symbolic of the crown-of-life promised to those who follow to the end the way of Christ.

65   Laurel Wreath: In medieval Europe, the laurel wreath came to be a symbol of prosperity, power and fame, as well as the certainty of the eternal life of a soul after death. St. Paul in 1 Corinthians likens Christian perseverance to running a race that requires rigorous discipline and practice, all for the glory of winning a wreath of laurel that will ultimately wither and die.

67   Unicorn: Drawn fom pre-Christian traditions, the unicorn is a beloved mythical creature that over time became a symbol of the incarnation, purity and the sinlessness of Jesus. This imaginary creature is represented in Christian art and iconography as a white horse with a long spiraled horn protruding from its forehead. Picturing a unicorn with its head in the lap of the Virgin Mary was common in medieval art.

69   Oil Lamp & Bible: An oil lamp stationed on a Bible has traditionally been interpreted as a symbol of guidance, knowledge and enlightenment; an understanding of the Word of God and a commitment to pursue the path of wisdom, righteous and the holiness it defines.

71   Crown of Thorns: Representing the chaplet of branches Jesus wore before and during his crucifixion, the crown of thorns is an especially evocative emblem, appropriately depicting the indignity nad shame to which Jesus was subjected when the soldiers braided a crown to mock him as a king of Jews. The plait of thorns takes the symbolic reference of the curse of the ground following the fall of man, and proclaims that Jesus has taken that curse upon himself.

73   Dogwood: In addition to its cruciform petals, Christians see in the dogwood blossom an illustration of several other aspects of the Passion of Christ.

75   Armenian Cross: Richly decorated, the motifs on Armenian crosses symbolize the life embodied in the cross itself, a life that flows freely from this otherwise ignominious instrument of death. Never bearing the body of Christ, Armenian crosses mirror some of the shapes and designs that were particularly favoured during the fourth century: clusters of grapes, vines, floral swirls, and accessories that had already appeared as engravings on the tombs of early Christians in the Roman catacombs.

77   Rooster: A common farmyard animal, the rooster, is a presage of the dawn and is interpreted as a symbol of the resurrection, and ultimately of Christ, who has scattered the darkness and invalidated the claim of death.

79   Star of Bethlehem: In Christian understanding, the Star of Bethlehem represents the heraldic, cosmic proclamation that Jesus has come in fulfilment of the prophetic Messianic promise. According to St. Matthew's Gospel, three wise men coming from the East saw a five-pointed star in the night sky that guided them to the Bethlehem grotto where the prophetic child was to be found. Although commonly associated with Christmas, this event is likely to have occurred a short time later. In western Christendom, the Feast of Epiphany celebrated on January 6 commemorates the momentous universal manifestation of God to humanity.

81   Greek Cross: Next to the Latin cross, the Greek cross is one of the most popular cruciforms in Christian expression. It is distinguished by an upright post with a transverse bar of equal length.

83   Chalice: Representing the most sacred moment in Christian worship when believers consume the sacramental wine that Jesus called the "blood of the covenant"—along with the bread to which Jesus referred as his body—the vessel has come to be treated with great respect, the chalice has traditionally been made of precious metal richly enameled and encrusted with jewels.

85   Pomegranate: Because of its plenitude of seeds, the pomegranate has long been used as a symbol of royalty, hope and future life. It is often used as a symbol of the Resurrection or of the church, where its seeds represent the many believers who make up the church universal.

87   Orthodox Cross: Of the more than four hundred variations of the Christian cross, each representing a vision of the central insignia of the Passion, the Eastern Orthodox cross is recognizably distinct. The Orthodox cruciform is distinguished by its three cross beams. The top arm could be called the Pontius Pilate bar, while the lower beam could represent a footrest for the crucified body of Christ.

89   Shamrock: According to legend, St. Patrick used the shamrock to explain to his listeners that this three-leaf clover was an image of the Holy Trinity: one God existing in perfect unity in three Persons of Father, Son and Holy Spirit.

91   Phoenix: Received and baptized into Christian iconography, the phoenix continues today to proclaim the doctrine of the resurrection of Jesus and of the ultimate resurrection of those who "fall asleep in Christ."

93   Alpha & Omega: Derived directly from the book of Revelation in which Jesus is quoted as saying, "I am the Alpha and the Omega," this symbol is a bold proclamation that Jesus the Messiah is the beginning and end of all things. In the language of the Nicene Creed of 325, Jesus the Messiah is declared, "God of God, Light of Light, Very God of Very God, begotten, not made, being of one substance with the Father by whom all things were made."

95   Palm Branches: Palm branches for christians call to mind the triumphal entry of Jesus into Jerusalem, the event that initiated his coming Passion and Crucifixion. Riding on a donkey, Jesus made a profound and unambiguous statement that the imminent events notwithstanding, he was indeed the Anointed One, the long awaited Messiah, the King of Israel, and the Saviour of all humankind, born to give birth to a new nation, a holy priesthood—the church.

97   Ankh: After its adoption by early Egyptian Christians, the Ankh was thoroughly Christianized and purged of its pagan associations, thereby becoming the central thematic symbol of Christian belief in Egypt and Ethiopia.

99   Serpent and Apple: When Christ is portrayed in Christina art holding an apple, he is understood to represent the second Adam, who brings salvation and eternal life to the world. The serpent, on the other hand, is generally regarded to be a crafty, malicious, and often deadly reptile, understood in the biblical context to have been the agent used by Satan to accomplish his malevolent work of temptation.

101 Ship at Sea: This image of the Church as a barque conveying the faithful between this world and the next was used by the early church Fathers when they referred to the Church as the Barque of Peter, with Peter the Fisherman as captain and helmsman.

103 Seven Doves: Seven descending doves surrounding a circle containing the letters "SS" (Sanctus Spiritus, Latin for Holy Spirit) forms the dramatic symbol used since ancient times for the gifts of the Holy Spirit enumerated in Isaiah

11:2-3. The gifts of the Holy Spirit the Messiah and his followers, were prophesied to embody were wisdom, understanding, right judgment, courage, knowledge, devotion, and fear of the Lord.

105 Sword and Bible: The sword is a symbol of divine authority and power. Portrayed on an open book, it represents the sword of the Spirit, or the word of truth—the gospel. It is also the emblem of many saints and martyrs who died by the sword. This link of the sword to the Bible occurs in the book of Hebrews in which the author notes that the Word of God is living, active, and sharper than any double-edged sword.

107 Censer: Deriving from Old Testament tradition, the liturgical practice in mainline and some Protestant churches of burning incense in a consecrated vessel and swinging it to distribute its fragrance is a rich symbol of blessing, consecration, and sanctification. Quite simply, incense is viewed and interpreted as a symbol of the intercessory prayers of God's people ascending to heaven—prayers that offer a promise to walk with Christ in the giving of themselves as a sacrifice to God for a sweet smelling fragrance (see Ephesians 5:2).

109 Olive Branch: For the Christian community, the olive branch is of particular consequence in denoting the peace offering of God brought to the world by Jesus Christ, who comes to us bearing the olive branch of God, the peace of the New Covenant.

111 Ewer and Basin: A ewer resting in a basin is a Christian symbol representing ritual purification and, more dramatically, calls to mind the gripping gesture of Jesus during the Supper when he knelt and washed the feet of the disciples.

113 Paschal (Easter) Egg: The egg was embraced by Christians as a joyful symbol of the Resurrection of Christ, and of the hope that believers have of their own rising from death to eternal life.

115 Cross Pattée: The most popular variation of the Pattée cross has arms of equal length, all of which narrow toward the centre, but are straight along the outer edge.

117 Messianic Seal of Jerusalem: The Messianic Seal of Jerusalem symbol, which did not come to public awareness until 1999, consists of a menorah—the most important symbol of Judaism—together with an outline of a vertical fish. The intersection of these two images forms a Star of David and together they comprise what was likely the most celebrated symbol of the first church in Jerusalem. The Seal is widely used by Jewish Christians who call themselves "Messianic Jews." The symbol is also enthusiastically embraced by many streams of evangelical Christian belief.

119 Advent Wreath: A season of reflection, inner preparation, expectation and hope, the wreath during Advent is a widely acknowledged and warmly welcomed symbol that anticipates the coming of the Christ child.

121 Jerusalem Cross: The standard Jerusalem Cross bearing four "Tau cross" arms is the central image of the Arms of the Knights and Dames of the Holy Sepulchre in Jerusalem, and is seen throughout Israel as a marking of the Franciscan order's custody of the Holy Land.

123 Poinsettia: The Advent wreath is a widely acknowledged and warmly welcomed symbol that anticipates not only the nativity of the Christ child, but the coming again of Jesus the Lord to consummate the faith and hope of the church. As a modern symbol of Advent, the poinsettia is the most popular plant of the Christmas season the world over, and is celebrated today for its star-shaped foliage which calls to mind the Star of Bethlehem.

125 Wheat: Wheat is the primary ingredient of bread, making the insistent claims of Jesus more comprehensible when he said, "I am the bread of life. He who comes to me will never go hungry, and he who believes in me will never be thirsty."

127 Sand Dollar: According to sand dollar legends, the shell was left by Christ as a teaching tool for evangelists of the faith to use in proclaiming the gospel.

129 Grapevine: Often depicted in clusters hanging on a vine, grapes are an expressly vivid symbol relating to the Holy Communion imagery of the Church. The vine represents Jesus, and the cluster of grapes that grows out of the vine expresses the Church to which Christ has given birth and which is inseparable from him.

131 Sun of Righteousness: In every sense and in every instance, Jesus is the fulfillment of all references in the Scriptures relating to the source and substance of light; he is the pinnacle and purpose of the acts of God in history; he ultimately is the culmination and summation of all created things.

133 Tongues of Fire: This second symbol of the Holy Spirit derives largely from the dramatic incident that occurs when the followers of Christ are anointed and baptized with Holy Spirit, these followers now becoming the Church as the Body of Christ.

135 Lyre: In the Book of Revelation the church is represented as celebrating the triumphs of redemption with music that "was like the sound of harpers playing on their harps" and singing a new song before the throne."

137 Bell: In Western tradition, the ringing of church bells is widely associated with the heralding of a joyous event, such as a wedding, a Christmas or Easter service to be celebrated in the church.

139 Creator's Star: The Star of David is an affirmation that the revelation of God that began with the Israel was an ongoing one, having as its point of culmination the Incarnation, the death and resurrection of Jesus.

141 Coptic Cross: Coptic Christians are fastidious in wearing the cross as a badge of association and as a statement of their faith in the sacrificial, atoning work of God in Christ, even when this blatant identification has the possibility of leading to martyrdom.

143 Skull: The use of the skull as a Christian symbol derives from the Gospel stories in which it is noted that Jesus was crucified between two thieves on a small hill called Gulgoleth, an Aramaic form of the Hebrew word meaning "Place of a Skull." These passages in the Gospels of Matthew, Mark, and John gave rise to the legend that Golgotha was the site of Adam's grave, and that the setting of the cross over the bones and skull of Adam was symbolic of Christ's blood flowing over the resting place of Adam, thereby cleansing him and his descendants from sin and bringing them into salvation in Christ. The skull lying at the foot of the cross on Golgotha is therefore symbolic of the skull of Adam receiving redemption through the victory of Christ over sin and death.

145 Daisy: The daisy is a late symbol of the innocence of the Christ Child. The daisy, less exotic and pretentious than the lily, was thought by some to be a more fitting symbol for the baby Jesus. By the late fifth century the religious connotation of the folksy and unassuming daisy was expressed as a fitting reference to the purity, humility and innocence of the Christ child.

147 Pearl: In specific reference to the warning Jesus gave to his disciples not to "throw pearls before swine," this lustrous offering of the clam or oyster has come to represent both the Kingdom of God and the Word of God.

149 Brazen Serpent: In the Gospel accounts, Jesus compares himself to the brazen serpen in the wilderness. and thereby authenticates the symbol of the serpent on the pole as a type of the Crucifixion.

151 Winged Man: Matthew is frequently represented in icons as a Winged Man, and occasionally in Christian art he is pictured with a book and a quill, ostensibly listening to an angel whispering the content of the sacred message the apostle is recording.

153 Keys of the Kingdom: The Keys of the Kingdom are a sacred trust from Christ to His church. Those keys symbolize custody of the very entrance to the Kingdom. He has . . . commanded us to preach the gospel so that we can stand as a beacon to point the way to that Kingdom.

155 Cross-Bearing Orb: This Christian symbol is essentially a globe surmounted by a cross as a representation of Christ's authority over the earth and all things temporal. As a symbol of authority and power, Christian monarchs have held an orb at their coronation. In Christian art, the Christ child sometimes holds an orb while seated on his Mother's lap.